Worship the King

Published by XP Publishing
A department of Christian Services Association
P.O. Box 1017, Maricopa, Arizona 85139
www.XPpublishing.com

ISBN: 978-1-936101-61-0

XPpublishing.com

Printed in the United States of America
For Worldwide Distribution

Worship the King

AN INSPIRING DEVOTIONAL THAT
DRAWS THE HEART INTO HIS PRESENCE

DEDICATED TO JESUS,

OUR SAVIOR, LORD, AND THE KING OF OUR HEARTS

CONTENTS

THE LORD IS WORTHY OF OUR WORSHIP. HE IS THE
KING OF ALL KINGS. THERE IS NO ONE LIKE HIM. HE IS
DAZZLING, GLORIOUS, AND AWESOME IN EVERY WAY.

MAY THIS DEVOTIONAL DRAW YOU INTO A LIFESTYLE OF
WORSHIP, FRIENDSHIP, AND INTIMACY

... WITH HIM!

Sing Me Like a Song:

A LIFESTYLE OF WORSHIP

Nic Billman

CHAPTER ONE

The Lord your God in your midst, The Mighty One, will
save; He will rejoice over you with gladness, He will quiet
you with His love, *He will rejoice over you with singing.*
—Zephaniah 3:17 NKJ, emphasis added—

CREATED IN HIS IMAGE

Do you realize that during the seven days of creation God created everything with the sound of His voice? God said, "Let there be light," and there was light. God said, "Let us create a firmament," and there was a firmament. As we read the creation story in Genesis, we see God speaking creation into existence. When He spoke, molecules began to vibrate and what was nothing became something. God created everything by the sound of His voice, except for you and me.

When God created man, He descended to the earth, got down on His knees and got His hands dirty as He reached into the dust to begin forming His most precious creation. Imagine the picture of God carefully molding and shaping man to be the mirror image of Himself. Each detail, each little line and curve was so important to Him. I picture God singing destiny over this, His most special creation, as He worked. When He was finished and man was molded and ready, you can almost see the proud smile of anticipation on God's face as He prepared to give life to His creation. Then God breathed His Spirit into the nostrils of the man. When Adam took his first breath and opened his eyes for the first time, he saw the face of his Creator, Father God. Adam was face-to-face with God in the paradise of His creation, the Garden of Eden.

Do you recall the first thing God told Adam to do? God created the animals, brought them to Adam, and said, "Name the animals." Why would God do that? Was it simply because He wanted to give Adam something to do until He created Eve? I believe it is because Adam was a son created in the image of his Father, not only in physical appearance, but also in his spiritual DNA; after all, God's breath gave Adam life.

God the Creator spoke all things into existence; likewise, Adam had the same ability to speak identity and destiny into creation. I am not suggesting that Adam was equal to God, but simply that Adam was like God in his ability to be creative. The enemy, who has no creative powers and can only steal, kill, and destroy, understood that you and I are to be creators and restorers, just like our Papa. This is why the lie of the serpent that deceived Eve was so tragic. Consider what he told her, "If you eat from this tree you'll be just like God." However, she was already like God because He had created her in His likeness. This is the same lie the religious use when they offer you by "works" that which is already yours through "inheritance" when you become a born-again child of God.

When we return to our place of being sons and daughters of the Living God, we are re-created in His image with the ability to speak identity and destiny into creation – into the lives of men and women, our families, our churches, and our cities. Your voice carries the reverberation of God's creative voice, and it has the power and authority to cast out darkness and replace it with light.

As sons and daughters of the Living God, we are re-created in His image with the ability to speak identity and destiny into creation. Your voice carries the reverberation of God's creative voice, and it has the power and authority to cast out darkness and replace it with light.

Ever since the Fall of man, God has been in the process of redeeming and restoring us to His original purpose, the one He spoke over us in the Garden of Eden. Just as then, He desires to talk with us and walk with us through the Garden. Our spiritual act of worship is for us to be living sacrifices maintaining a lifestyle of worship, walking hand-in-hand with our Papa through the garden of life, stepping between the flowers and thorns, speaking destiny and identity with each stride.

Thermostats vs. Thermometers

Recently we were in Santa Fe, New Mexico, and had an amazing encounter with Jesus in the middle of the city. We were with our dear friend, Alan Hawkins, who wanted to show us the Plaza in Santa Fe. The Plaza is a town square with a big yard, some trees, and a large monument in the center. It is a gathering place of both locals and tourists; a popular place to pray, play, or smoke weed. If you have never been to Santa Fe, you need to know that it is the New Age and spiritual capital of Western United States. There is a fusion of the New Age, Eastern religions, Wicca, and Native American spiritual beliefs.

While Alan parked the car, I noticed a guy playing a beat-up guitar and singing through a mike plugged into an amp, powered by a car battery, with a hat in front of him to collect money. He was singing a mixture of '60s folk songs and his own original music. When he took a break, I went over and asked if I could play a song. At first he was hesitant, but when I slipped him a twenty-dollar bill, he happily obliged.

When I started playing, Rachael came over to join me. We sang a song that we wrote, called "Sing Me Like a Song." If you did not know us, you might think that it was just a simple love song. As we sang, a crowd gathered and people began putting money in the man's hat. When the song was over I thanked him and started to give him his guitar, but as a smart businessman who saw the money overflowing from the hat, he asked us to do another song.

The second song we sang is called "Shores of Grace." Again, if you did not know the reason we write music, you could think it is just a beautiful song about a father and his love. One of the things I like about the people in the New Age is that they are very open to other religions and any positive spirit. As we sang, the crowd grew even larger. Once again, after the song, I tried to give the guitar back, but he was counting the money and he said, "Keep playing!" This time we did a song called "The Invitation." This song, unlike the others, clearly identifies for whom it was written. At one point in the song, we declare the name of Jesus three times. I want to share the lyrics of that song with you.

The Invitation

by Nic and Rachael Billman

I see the light coming from the throne

Breaking through the night as You call.

I feel the trembling

The trembling of the dark

At each mention of Your name,

Jesus, Jesus, Jesus.

Come up here, come up here,

My beloved, my bride.

I hear the cries, the cries of a broken bride

And I long to hold you in My arms

As we dance.

I've taken away the stained and filthy rags

That you once called identity.

And I have laid out garments of white

Sewn with grace and washed in blood.

Come up here, come up here,

My beloved, my bride.

The Spirit and the bride say come.

The Spirit and the bride say come.

The Spirit and the bride say come.

As we sang, you could feel the atmosphere thickening with the presence of the Holy Spirit. When we came to the part of the song where we speak the name, "Jesus," hands went up all around the Plaza and some began to weep. It was a powerful encounter with Jesus! Think about it, people of the New Age, Eastern religions, and witchcraft were worshipping the name of Jesus. Do you know what all of those people had in common? They were all seekers, and Jesus promises that if we seek Him, we *will* find Him. Although they are disconnected from God, they too were created by His hand and breath. They may not know it, because it is hidden deep within their spirits, but inside they have a longing for the Father. They were responding to the sound of the Father.

After we finished, we thanked the man and returned his guitar. As we got up to leave, several people from the crowd greeted us. One guy with long dreadlocks who was sporting the unique fragrance of marijuana said, "Thank you. That was such a positive spirit." I hugged him and said, "You have no idea how positive He is." Several other people simply asked, "What was that?" We told them, "It's Jesus and He loves you very much." One young lady asked Rachael to pray with her. She was a vocalist who had been dabbling in Hinduism but had not felt at peace for a long time. She said that when we sang, she felt peace return to her. Rachael had a chance to pray with her and share a prophetic word that God had for her. The girl wept and wept, and she gave her heart to Jesus. Then she smiled, and her radiant smile was beautiful.

Do you understand what happened at the Plaza that day? We worshipped the Father, He came and inhabited our praise, and the atmosphere changed. He did not call you and me to be thermometers; we were created to be thermostats. Thermometers are passive, they simply gauge the temperature, but thermostats are active and change the temperature. It is very easy to look at a place like that and say, "Oh, wow, look at this mixture of different religions, look at all of these false gods and evil practices." That requires no talent or spiritual gifting.

God did not create you to list all that is wrong in an atmosphere; He created you to change the atmosphere. Think about what Jesus did. Jesus looked and saw with the eyes of the Father and then changed atmospheres with His compassion, with His words, and by healing their diseases. God called you and me to be *thermostats*.

ULTIMATE TUNING FORK

Rachael and I love to use new and unique sounds in worship. God is the creator of sound and we love to discover new ways to direct sound back to Him through our worship. One of our favorites is crystal singing bowls. They are crafted from pure crystal, cut and tuned perfectly to the key of your choice, and the sound they make is absolutely gorgeous. To produce a tone, you hit the side of the bowl with a padded mallet and slowly drag the mallet around the edge of the bowl. It is similar to running a damp finger around the top of a crystal glass.

God did not create you to list all that is wrong in an atmosphere; He created you to change the atmosphere. God called you and me to be thermostats.

These bowls were created originally to stimulate the chakras, which comes from the Hindu belief that our bodies have seven energy centers that are in tune with seven different notes. They believe that when you play that note, it clears up blockages in that "chakra" or area of your body and there is healing. My belief is similar in some ways but very different in others! I believe that when we direct our music and songs to God in worship, it creates an atmosphere of freedom and healing. Not because a specific instrument or note brings healing, but because God inhabits the praises of His people (see Psalm 22:3) and "where the Spirit of the Lord is, there is freedom" (2 Corinthians 3:17 NCV).

We have seen many divine healings during worship – both physical and emotional. Recently during worship, a man who had been mute for seven years because of a stroke began to speak as God touched him. I believe that the chakra practice was originally a revelation that came from God but that the enemy distorted. We have to remember that Lucifer was the director of music in heaven. Consequently, two of his favorite practices are destroying atmospheres of worship and distorting revelation concerning music and worship. This is why many of the disagreements in church center around styles of music and worship.

Not long after we received the bowls, we were in Santa Fe and had our encounter at the Plaza. We were to minister at a church in the city that evening. At the end of our worship time, Rachael and I played the crystal bowls and a beautiful thing happened. At first, there was absolute silence. Then the first bowl chimed "dong" and the deep sound swelled and began to grow. Then the second bowl, in a higher octave, chimed "dong," and the sound of the two bowls filled the silence in the room. After a minute or two, a woman began to sing in the Spirit along with the bowls. Within five minutes, everyone in the room was singing in the Spirit in perfect harmony with the bowls.

God has always been singing to us, and the
greatest song He ever sang was Jesus.

It was a beautiful and holy moment. Then the Holy Spirit, the Teacher, began to pour revelation into my heart. I heard Him say, "These bowls are just like Jesus. He was sent to bring the sons and daughters, and all of creation, into harmony with the Father."

You see, Jesus was a song that God sang over the earth. God has always been singing to us, and the greatest song He ever sang was Jesus.

When He sent Jesus to earth, it was not only die for our sins and redeem us, but it was also to show us how to live. He sent Jesus to be the ultimate tuning fork to give us the perfect tone, pitch, or key by which to live. As the writer of Hebrews put it, we are to look to Jesus, the author and finisher of our faith (see Hebrews 12:2). He was the perfect song sung by the Father to bring His children back to Him. Even on the Cross, He sang to us in sweet surrender. Once we hear the song of Jesus, we fall in love with Him and join in the song, and that is the greatest duet that can ever exist – the Bridegroom and the Bride singing in harmony the love song of salvation and redemption.

Recently, we visited a rescue home for children near us in Brazil in a city known for prostitution. Eighteen girls, ranging in ages from one to eighteen, lived in this particular house. After a time of visiting and sharing, we moved out to the porch and spent some time in worship. As I played the guitar, I watched these girls cry tears of joy and sing love songs to Jesus, thanking Him for saving them. Many of their families sold them into prostitution for as little as five dollars worth of crack cocaine. They were raped an average ten times a night, beaten, abused, molested, and in some cases left for dead.

Yet, there they were, singing their hearts out, thanking Jesus for His goodness and mercy. The director of the house told us that they earnestly pray for forgiveness and the redemption of the people who abused them. Why would they do that? Because they are not only rescued, they have been redeemed. They have tasted the freedom found in Jesus and want others to experience the same freedom, even those who caused their bondage and pain. They have come into perfect harmony with the redemption song of Jesus and they sing it daily, not just with their mouths but also with their lives.

Earlier, I mentioned that we wrote a song titled, "Sing Me Like a Song," and I would like to share the lyrics with you. John Wimber, the founder of the Vineyard movement, said something that I love: "God, I want to be a coin in Your pocket, spend me however You want." What a simple, yet profound prayer! As a musician, my prayer is, "God let me be a song in Your heart, sing me however You want." As you read the lyrics, you may want to make it your prayer as well.

Once we hear the song of Jesus, we fall in love with Him and join in the song, and that is the greatest duet that can ever exist – the Bridegroom and the Bride singing in harmony the love song of salvation and redemption.

Sing Me Like a Song

by Nic and Rachael Billman

The sound of a thousand dove's wings in flight

The sound of many waters rushing over and o'er

The sound of heaven's keys dancing in the night

The sound of a Father, the song of a Son

The roar of a Lion, the breath of a Lamb

The sound of the harvest receiving the wind

My lover, I am Yours.

So sing me like a song.

However and whenever you want

Just sing me like a song.

The sound of your breakers colliding the shore

The cry of the deep, the beckon of love

The shackles and chains falling down to the floor

The sound of your heartbeat calling me home

The sound of our tears filling bottles of clay

The dropping of blood on stones meant for us

My lover, I am Yours.

So sing me like a song.

However and whenever You want

Just sing me like a song.

Worship Is More than You Think

JONATHAN WILLIAMS

CHAPTER TWO

Now to the King eternal, immortal, invisible, the only God, be honor and glory forever and ever.

—1 Timothy 1:17—

The God we serve is holy, wonderful, loving, pure, good, faithful, true, glorious... I could go on for the entire chapter speaking of who God is and why He is so wonderful. As worshippers, we need to refresh our minds constantly of the goodness of God. We are not trying to convince ourselves of this truth, but we are reminding ourselves because we never want to forget or take for granted how amazing our God is.

WORSHIP, A CHILD'S ONLY HOPE

Looking back on my childhood, I realize that I reminded myself of God's goodness on a regular basis. For part of my adolescent years, I lived with my grandparents because of my mother's drug addiction. My sister and I grew up watching my mother take drugs, sell them, and suffer physical abuse from her boyfriend. These are the most traumatic moments of my life but also the most precious times I ever experienced. This is when I discovered the presence of God, and it became my escape from all the bad things in my life. I was at church worshipping God at every opportunity because I knew that only God could rescue my mother, my sister, and me from the hell in which we lived.

Praying nearly every day for a change in my mother's lifestyle brought my mother to the moment when she had to make a decision to get clean or lose everything, including her children. God provided a way for her to go to a facility for a few years to get clean and get her life straightened out. During that time, my sister and I lived with my grandparents. It was a blessing in disguise because those years propelled me into a life of worship and adoration of my Savior, Jesus Christ.

I am a living testimony that God's Word is true; He really causes "all things to work together for good to those who love God, to those who are called according to His purpose" (Romans 8:28). I have always known that God had a special calling on my life and that He wants to use me for a very special purpose. Through that difficult time, I learned how to love the Lord God with all my heart, soul, and mind. I learned that it was not "all about me" but about learning to turn my heart and focus to the One worthy of all my affections.

LOVE HIM WITH ALL YOUR HEART
You shall love the Lord your God *with all your heart* (Luke 10:27).

When we love the Lord with all of our heart, we love Him with all of our desires, aspirations, and dreams. In the natural, our heart is a vital organ that keeps us alive, pumping blood throughout our body. In the spiritual, our heart is much the same; it circulates God's love to every area of our being. Loving God with our heart is synonymous with worshipping Him.

I believe our outward expression of worship reflects our inward relationship with Jesus. What is in your heart? Is it filled with a wonderful desire to please your Savior, your God, and your Friend? Take a moment to examine your heart to discover what is there. Pray Psalm 139:23, "Search me, O God, and know my heart; test me and know my anxious thoughts" (NIV).

Our outward expression of worship reflects our inward relationship with Jesus. What is in your heart? Is it filled with a wonderful desire to please your Savior, God, and Friend?

We know from Scripture that the heart can be wicked and corrupt, but we also know that we are new creatures in Christ. We have literally had a change of heart. God takes out our wicked, hard heart and replaces it with a new heart when we give Him our lives. The Father wants to give us *His* heart, *His* desire for an intimate relationship.

Worship is so much more than singing a few songs during a service. In fact, worship does not require singing at all. God wants our hearts fully engaged with His. He wants us to love Him with *all* of our heart, and that requires keeping our desires and dreams focused on Him. When His truth engages our hearts, we are able to worship God on a much deeper level.

The extent of our knowledge of God (through His Word and by experiencing Him) is the level to which we will be able to worship Him in Spirit and in Truth.

LOVE HIM WITH ALL YOUR MIND

You have probably heard the saying, "The mind is a beautiful thing." Yes, it can be a very beautiful thing, especially since we have access to the mind of Christ when we give our life to Him. My wife tells me that I am analytical. I know there has to be a balance, but I believe this trait is from God and that He wants me to love Him with my *entire* mind, even the logical part: "You shall love the Lord your God … with *all your mind*" (Luke 10:27).

This Scripture not only means to keep your mind clean from sin, but also to go beyond what people tell you about God to discover a more personal truth. Could this Scripture also be saying we should use our intelligence to dig into His Word and search Him out? When the Word of God renews our mind, it also upgrades our understanding of God with a fresh outlook. Because we are developing the mind of Christ, our old mind, our former understanding and attitudes are going away. Therefore, we are learning a new way to think:

> Whatever things are true, whatever things *are* noble, whatever things *are* just, whatever things *are* pure, whatever things *are* lovely, whatever things *are* of good report, if *there is* any virtue and if *there is* anything praiseworthy— meditate on these things (Philippians 4:8 NKJV).

Loving the Lord with all your mind is crucial to your relationship with the Father. As we worship Him, He pours out revelation to our spirit. However, our mind is the way we process that fresh revelation. We will not always understand the ways of the Lord,

The extent of our knowledge of God (through His Word and by experiencing Him) is the level to which we will be able to worship Him in Spirit and in Truth.

because they are not our ways and His thoughts are higher than our thoughts. But, He has given us a mind to use in pursuing Him. With renewed minds, we can think upon His truths and worship Him as we begin to understand with our intellect how amazing and beautiful He is.

Love Him with All Your Strength

You shall love the Lord your God ... *with all your strength* (Luke 10:27).

As director of The School of Worship at Teen Mania Ministries in Garden Valley, Texas, I have come to understand this area of loving the Lord with my strength in a whole new way. During the first two weeks of a new school year, we have what we call corporate exercise. The entire student body and staff come together and exercise from 6 to 7 a.m. I am not a person who enjoys getting up early to work out (and it shows). However, as I got up each morning to exercise with the class, I began to see that it is important to have the physical strength to serve God throughout my day. Taking care of the temple of the Holy Spirit (the body) has taken on new meaning to me.

The times of corporate exercise not only stretched my physical strength but also opened my eyes to the meaning of continually worshiping God. While it is wonderful to be on stage and sing to the Lord, we must also worship Him *at all times*. This exercise gave

God is looking for those whose hearts are fully His. He
is looking for those who will love and worship Him with
everything within them – including their physical strength.

me the opportunity to check myself spiritually, to see what came
out of me when I was tired, sore, and wishing I were back in bed.
I do not believe that failing to exercise every morning disqualifies
you from being a worshipper. However, God is looking for those
whose hearts are fully His. Our ability to operate on a physical level
is important to God and He is looking for those who will love and
worship Him with everything within them – including their physical strength.

WORSHIPPING BRINGS GOD'S PRESENCE

Being a worshipper is not only about singing, playing an instrument, waving a flag, or lifting hands. A worshipper is someone
who carries the presence of God everywhere they go. When people
talk to you in the grocery store, at your place of work, and other
places you go, they should notice something different about you,
because the very presence of God dwells inside you. They may not
say anything, but your presence should plant a seed of hope and
joy in their heart.

Being a worshipper also means that you bless and serve the
Lord at all times. Giving your heart, mind, and strength to Him
on a daily basis is pivotal to being a true worshipper of Christ.
Worshiping is not merely a form of religion; it actually puts action
to your faith – make a choice to serve God and love Him with everything inside of you every day, all day.

Lastly, blessing people is a big part of being a worshipper. God is looking for people to represent Him. That means to literally *re-present* Him to others.

Those who learn to worship God with their heart, soul, and mind will demonstrate Christ in every area of their lives to a world looking for "something" that can only be found in Someone – God.

THE *AS* OF WORSHIP

BISHOP JOSEPH L. GARLINGTON, SR.

CHAPTER THREE

Let my prayer be counted *as* incense before you, and the
lifting up of my hands *as* the evening sacrifice!
                    —Psalm 141:2 ESV, emphasis added—

Nothing in my hands I bring…
                    —Augustus Toplady's *Rock of Ages*—

When the word *as* is used adverbially, it tends to
convey equivalency or equality in its comparative
use. In this great Psalm a marvelous truth of worship is revealed – physical actions can become
spiritual realities.

One of our deepest insights into worship comes from a conversation between Jesus and a marginalized and rejected Samaritan

woman. In this poignant moment, Jesus is about to do what His mother prophesied shortly after she conceived Him: "He has filled the hungry with good things, and the rich he has sent away empty" (Luke 1:53 ESV). The Samaritan woman is hungry, and He is about to fill her to overflowing.

She had just shared her concept of Samaritan worship in contrast to its Jewish counterpart: It is a *place*. Her idea of *place* is on Mount Gerizim, where Sanballat built their temple more than three centuries earlier. The Jews' *place* is on Mount Zion, where Herod built the temple forty-six years prior. Jesus summarily discards *both* paradigms by saying that in the immediate future neither will be the epicenter for worship.

He informs her that the basic substance of worship is not *place* but *spirit*. "God is spirit," He says, "and those who worship him must worship in spirit and truth" (John 4:24 ESV). With these words, He is revealing to her that true worship is first of all a spiritual reality. One lexicon informs us that the Greek word translated *truth* is "aletheia," and it speaks of "the unveiled reality lying at the basis of and agreeing with an appearance; the manifested, the veritable essence of a matter."[1]

In some wonderful and mysterious way, a simple physical action in worship can have greater implications in the spiritual dimension than we can possibly imagine.

Reason and sense dominate the Western world and we who live there are often oblivious and ignorant of what much of the rest of the world believes about the unseen world. The church often does not live from a supernatural worldview, and it tends to discard concepts that jar our sensibilities and dignity. This, however, was not the world of the Old or New Testament; these people

In some wonderful and mysterious way, a simple physical action in worship can have greater implications in the spiritual dimension than we can possibly imagine.

were comfortable with two realities – the seen and unseen. A vast majority of those who live in the other two-thirds of the world—a dimension steeped in spiritual darkness concerning God's kingdom and His Son—are very much aware of an unseen dimension, and it is often a part of their day-to-day existence.

When anyone is introduced to the Kingdom of God, they enter a spiritual dimension that can only be apprehended by the Spirit. Jesus told the scholarly Pharisee, Nicodemus, that the ability to participate in this sphere is only possible when one is "born of water and the Spirit." The problem then, as now, is the theological baggage that often obscures and/or downplays the existence of an unseen world of invisible creatures with supernatural powers.

In recent years, sincere missionaries from the West have been forced to make drastic paradigm shifts in long-standing theories of world missions and evangelism. Their new worldview of missions has required a radical adjustment in practice when they come face-to-face with issues that were not merely cultural differences but rather a clash between two opposing spiritual kingdoms. Some, in their unwillingness to embrace these very real matters, use theological arguments to either marginalize or eliminate the problem. However, by doing this, they fabricate a structure that holds to a "form" of religion while "denying" its power.

PRECEDENTS OFTEN REVEAL OR ESTABLISH A PRINCIPLE

"Let my prayer be counted *as* incense before you" (Psalm 141:2 ESV). This Psalm has a historical context. David is facing two very real, basic needs in his life. The first one is his need to survive, and the other, which for David is just as important, is the need to worship. At this critical time in his life, staying alive is David's day-by-day priority. He informed Jonathan, his covenant brother, "There is but a step between me and death" (1 Samuel 20:3 ESV). In spite of this, what David seems to desire most is participation in the worship that takes place at the altar every morning and evening.

However, David has a problem – he is unable to bring the daily sacrifices God required of the worshipping community. He has no altar at which to sacrifice, and since he is not a Levite he would be unqualified to offer those sacrifices. He has no one-year-old lamb to sacrifice, the sacred incense for the burnt offerings is forbidden for personal use, and he has no certainty where he will be the next day.

Saul, when newly anointed king, presumed that his position qualified him to offer a sacrifice and that act disqualified him from a continuing reign. David, on the other hand, sought to improvise worship. He made a request of God that revealed a principle of worship which would be established for millennia and become the basis of worship in our day.

David humbly requested Almighty God to accept his current predicament – an inability to bring the worship God required – and allow Him to offer a substitute that would have equal value. When God instructed Moses and Aaron as to what constituted accept-able worship, He gave them detailed instructions about what could be offered, when it could be offered, where it could be offered, and who was authorized to do these things. Our understanding of Scripture does not explain the full meaning behind these items.

Worship is first and foremost a supernatural experience that can only be entered by faith. Faith is the obedient response to the commands that God gives His children. Hidden in mystery is *why* God requires us to bring to Him certain things. For example, we must accept as inevitable the truth that we will never be able to plumb the depths of the real reason God rejected Cain's offering and accepted Abel's. There are yet "the secret things" that "belong to the Lord our God" (Deuteronomy 29:29 ESV), that He has chosen not to reveal to us. His ways are "higher" than our ways and His thoughts infinitely superior. I am convinced that our outward expressions of worship are veiled as to why they were "chosen" by God in the first place.

Jesus queried the learned Nicodemus, "If I have told you earthly things and you do not believe, how can you believe if I tell you heavenly things?" (John 3:12 ESV). The writer of Hebrews says the accouterments of worship in the Old Testament were copies of heavenly things. Let us recognize that while God has shrouded these activities in mystery, He has not excluded us from receiving the graces that come by faith when we approach Him. Like the iceberg, the submerged part we do not see is an even greater reality than the one visible to us. I believe that David fully embraced these unseen mysteries and later, in his journey as king of Israel, we will see this passion expressed in many other ways.

In light of the foregoing, let's consider the significance of the seemingly unimportant two-letter word *as* that is found in our text. "Let my prayer be counted *as* incense before you, and the lifting up of my hands *as* the evening sacrifice!" (Psalm 141:2 ESV). Remember, the dictionaries tell us that when the word *as* is used adverbially, it tends to convey equivalency or equality in its comparative use. Now we know that David is making a bold and amazing request of God – he needs to improvise worship and is desperate for the Lord's permission.

His request actually goes beyond a mere human understanding of the divine mystery of the burnt offerings or the incense offering. He is requesting that God, at the time of the evening sacrifice, accept his raised hands as a substitute for the burnt offering (see Exodus 29:38–30:8). Let me paraphrase David's request of Psalm 141:2.

> God, in whatever way those offerings have meaning to You, please let my lifted hands have the same value. May my lifted hands be equal to an actual lamb slain at the evening sacrifice. May my prayer have the same elements and be equal to the incense offering, and when You hear it, let it be as pleasingly fragrant as the incense.

Is David tapping into the primitive awakening of a prophetic worship principle hidden in the Torah? Is this a divine revelation that informs David's worshipping heart of the reality of *spirit* worship? Is the Holy Spirit giving him an unconscious intuition of the event the apostle John will witness, thousands of years later, when he visits heaven? John discovered that the prayers of the saints are no longer *as* incense, but they *are* incense. As Jehovah grants this amazing request, He allows a precedent to be established for all believers who lack access to the God-ordained trappings of worship.

I believe David's courage to make this request of the Lord comes from an understanding of the Law and knowledge that, in other cases, Jehovah has made similar rulings. One clear example of this principle is the Lord's action concerning the tithe of the Levites found in Numbers 18:25–30. God commanded Moses to instruct the Levites that a tenth of the tithe presented to Him will "count" in equal value and volume in His sight as though they gave the "fullness" of the winepress:

> And the Lord spoke to Moses, saying, "Moreover, you shall speak and say to the Levites, 'When you take from the people of Israel the tithe that I have given you from them for your inheritance, then you shall present a contribution from it to the Lord, a tithe of the tithe. And your contribution shall be counted to you *as though* it were the grain of the threshing floor, and *as* the fullness of the winepress (Numbers 18:25-27 ESV, emphasis added).

A synecdoche is a figure of speech in which a part represents the whole. One of the real mysteries of worship is expressed in the question, "What is the whole behind the earthly symbols or the parts of worship?" The "parts" are the things visible to us in our dimension that are immeasurably powerful in the invisible and eternal dimension.

God wants His people to know that their obedience in bringing Him their tithe—whatever it might be—would be *as though* it was equal—in His sight—to the full volume of grain on the threshing floor from which it originated. In whatever way God regarded the "fullness of the winepress," He says, "I will allocate to your offering the same value."

By comparison to the *infinite*, these *finite* small parts play a significant role in the complete fabric of worship in the universe as Divine intelligence "works all things according to the counsel of his will" (Ephesians 1:11 ESV).

We find another example of this principle later in the Old Testament, when a seemingly innocuous action in the natural and visible sphere carried great weight in the supernaturally invisible one. When the prophet Elisha was dying, Joash, the king of Israel, visited him. Elisha made an unusual request, that Joash shoot an arrow out of a window opened toward the east. There was no explanation or reason given for the request, but the king complied. Elisha then revealed to him that his symbolic action performed in obedience procured for him a future and decisive victory over the Syrians.

This unusual request was followed by another. The king was to take his arrows and strike the ground. When the king only struck the ground three times, Elisha was angered and informed the king that his passivity had kept him from total victory over his enemy (see 2 Kings 13:14–19). It is unfortunate that the king was not discerning enough to seize the moment for further victories and missed a crucial opportunity for the total defeat of his enemies.

Paul told the church at Rome, "Whatever was written in former days was written for our instruction" (Romans 15:4 ESV). What does the Holy Spirit want us to learn from Joash's experience in Elisha's bedroom? What can we, the twenty-first century church, discover from this verse that is as critically strategic to our advancement today as it was for this king thousands of years ago?

One of my favorite quotes is from the movie, *Field of Dreams*. It represents a truism for much of the Christian church and worshipping community:

Quantum physicists have long contended that tiny, subatomic actions eventually have huge outcomes at great distances from their point of inception; and this is certainly true in the invisible spiritual world.

"You know, we just don't recognize the most significant moments of our lives while they are happening."

I believe the story of Elisha and the king would tell us that God will do new things but His people may not perceive them.

Many in our communities of worship and intercession are familiar with the concept of "prophetic actions." We believe these are "pantomimes" divinely orchestrated by the Holy Spirit to accomplish an unseen end in the purposes of God. Many times we are not told what that purpose is, and we must be content to live in the tension of walking by faith and not by sight. Prophetic actions in Scripture are many and varied, often indicating that something greater than the physical action is being accomplished.

Quantum physicists have long contended that tiny, subatomic actions eventually have huge outcomes at great distances from their point of inception, and this is so true in the invisible spiritual world.

Much of what we do in worship has a greater hidden significance than we have yet to understand, primarily because we have embraced the *visible* practice without recognizing or acknowledging the hidden mystery underlying the action. Today we sing the phrase from the hymn, "Rock of Ages," "*Nothing* in my hand I bring." However, in Lamentations 3:41 we read, "Let us lift up our heart with our hands unto God in the heavens" (KJV). This indicates I *can* bring something to God in my hands. Much later in David's life, he acknowledged that, "The sacrifices of God are a broken spirit; a broken and contrite heart" (Psalm 51:17 ESV).

A New Altar

> We have an altar from which those who serve the tent have no right to eat (Hebrews 13:10 ESV).

I have long contended that King David was not an Old Testament worshipper, yet it is clear that he functioned comfortably as a prophet, priest, and a king. He made extraordinary innovations to the old covenant worship paradigm. In fact, at face value, he violated the Aaronic law of the priesthood, yet seemed absolutely at ease with his actions. A thousand years later, Jesus Christ Himself justified one of David's many "out of the box" actions when confronting the Pharisees:

> He said to them, "Have you not read what David did when he was hungry, and those who were with him: how he entered the house of God and ate the bread of the Presence, which it was not lawful for him to eat nor for those who were with him, but only for the priests?" (Matthew 12:3–4 ESV).

Through David's example, believers in every generation are given permission to see their frail human actions as having incalculable value in the sight of God. David was living by the principle of worship Jesus taught – in spirit and truth. He validated this principle a thousand years before it was enunciated by Christ, and it shows modern worshippers how through faith, innovation, and confidence, we can enjoy greater depth and substance in our sometimes seemingly "feeble" acts of worship.

Hebrews informs us that the Melchizedek priesthood forever changed the law of worship. We no longer come in fear, we come boldly. We now know that our actions in worship actually count for something, and we may conclude that we are part of an innumerable company, visible and invisible, who by the wisdom of God, will see the "knowledge of the glory of the Lord [cover the earth] as the waters cover the sea!" (Habakkuk 2:14 NIV).

---

[1] Zodhiates, S. (2000). *The Complete Word Study Dictionary: New Testament* (electronic ed.). Chattanooga, TN: AMG Publishers.

A New Wave

BRIAN WRIGHT

CHAPTER FOUR

I have been the worship leader at Gateway Church for a little over ten years. At the age of twelve, I began playing an electric guitar and singing the old hymns with my mother and father in a small church of about fifty. Some of the wells dug many years ago in worship will never lose their power! I played guitar in the worship band at Gateway for seven years before being put in charge of praise and worship. Even though being a worship leader was my destiny, God wanted me to go through a time of spiritual seasoning before stepping into my future.

DEADLY DETOUR

In spite of being in church all my life and being established in a deep understanding of God, when I became a teenager I rebelled against God and the church and began experimenting with drugs and alcohol. I continued using my musical talent but not in praise and worship, rather with classic rock and roll. God had a destiny for me and the enemy saw that destiny and attempted to sidetrack me.

Finally, I reached a point where if change did not occur, I would end up dead or in prison. I truly believe that the tough experiences of my youthful years gave me much of the passion I draw upon in worship today, both personally and while leading others. During worship, I often see flashes of where my life was headed when I was away from Him, and that makes me more appreciative of what He has brought me through. My soul cries tears of gladness – I cannot contain the abundant mercy He has shown me. My thankfulness flows out of my spirit into songs of worship.

FLASHES OF DESTINY

During worship, God began to show me the destinies of other people as they worship, and prophetic words flow as He creates a glorious prophetic atmosphere.

The songs I love the most are those developed by God as we open our hearts and minds to His thoughts. This kind of worship goes beyond notes and words. During these times, God is actually directing the worship, and I become an instrument He plays.

One of the reasons our worship services have become so powerful is because of the freedom given to me by our senior pastors, who allow me to go where I sense the Holy Spirit is leading. When God has full reign in worship, signs, miracles, and wonders have a resting place, and it becomes a safe place for the prophetic to reside. I would encourage senior pastors to trust their worship leaders and allow them the freedom to move as the Holy Spirit leads.

There will be an influx of people to our churches in these last days who crave more than a pre-packaged program. They will desire a true encounter with the King of Glory.

God is changing how we do church — to be the church He desires today, we need to change with Him! The same pre-packaged version of church — four songs, offering, and a sermon — is not enough anymore.

There will be an influx of people to our churches in these last days who crave more than a pre-packaged program. They will desire a true encounter with the King of Glory and worship will be a tool God uses to bring them into His presence.

With the atmosphere of freedom I was given, God conveyed to me where He wanted to take the worship at Gateway Church. He spoke to me about a night devoted entirely to worship, a time when His people come together simply to give Him praise and worship. No agendas or preaching — just a time when believers would praise Him for who He is, what He has done, and what He is about to do.

The Wave

This was the birthing of "The Wave." The Wave meets the last Friday of every month. We begin with worship and allow God to have His way. We wait upon Him to direct us in what He wants to do. It is called "The Wave" because that is a good description of how God often moves in a corporate setting.

Picture the ocean in your thoughts. You have probably seen how ocean waves sweep upon the beach and then draw back while the next wave is strengthening to wash ashore. When God's glory falls, it often comes in waves. A wave of His glory will roll in, subside a little, you sense another wave building, and then a new one washes over you again.

When God's glory falls, it often comes in waves. A wave of His glory will roll in, subside a little, you sense another wave building, and then a new one washes over you again.

Wave nights are never alike. God may want to heal people in one Wave and, in another, speak prophetically through people. We never try to recreate what God did in a previous meeting. He always changes it and keeps us guessing as to what He will do next. It is just like God to cause us to seek Him for what He wants, rather than what we think should take place.

Destiny Mobilization

Simply stated, God will be as big a part of worship services as He is allowed to be. He gives us a choice: allow Him complete freedom and receive all He has for us, or settle for something less.

The Wave has become a blessing to Northeast Ohio as many denominations come together to worship the Lord. It has grown over the years and become a tool for equipping many who are thirsty for freedom in worship. People come from all over the region to experience the freedom that reigns at The Wave. Often they go home and begin their own Wave-like services.

God has incrementally revealed His purpose for The Wave. During great times of worship and praise, God has healed many and filled people with the Holy Spirit. Prophetic words have come to life through praise, causing lives to be changed and people to be equipped for service.

God has expanded our vision and has begun to make mobilization a part of The Wave. We have had great praise, worship, and equipping; however, now God is telling us that it is time to engage in bringing God's Kingdom to earth. (Let me say "thank you" to Patricia King for helping reveal this activation to me as I was seeking direction from God.)

A word from the Lord came to us that The Wave was to send a mission team to Cambodia to join the effort to end child slavery in the sex trade. One of the maxims of our ministry is "incremental implementation," but this word from God about the mission trip blew that right out of the water. Nothing like diving into mobilization headfirst! I love soaking in His Spirit and hanging out with Him on a Wave night, but our relationship with God is about more than enjoying His presence. He has a Great Commission for us to fulfill.

The deposits of His glory we receive during worship are to empower us to mobilize and multiply God's Kingdom on the earth.

Developers of Destiny

As worship leaders, we are to develop others in their callings to lead praise and worship. If you visit The Wave or a Sunday morning worship service, you will see various people leading the songs. The Holy Spirit uses me to help coordinate the people He commissions to lead worship – those who guide others into the Throne Room. We have many different individuals, of various ages, leading worship.

Yes, our worship leaders are all ages. This is a season for placing the youth in prominent positions during times of worship and praise. I believe our ceiling should be their floor; they start where we are and then surpass us in worship. I believe young people

> The deposits of His glory we receive during
> worship are to empower us to mobilize and
> multiply God's Kingdom on the earth.

should be an integral part of regular praise teams, standing side by side with the current generation. By including them, we create an intertwining of the worship anointing on the present and future generations.

The youth of today are hearing a new sound from heaven that God is releasing on the earth – I want that new sound in our worship times! Having them on stage also allows an impartation of wisdom and knowledge that they can apply to their own services. A great example of the new sound young people have tapped into is the music coming out of Hillsong United and Jesus Culture. They have helped introduce new sounds from heaven that call down the glory of God and bring a new freedom to worship. This sound, I believe, will bring in the last great revival that ushers in the coming of the King of Glory.

Nothing that has taken place at The Wave and Gateway Church is because of any individual. It is a result of allowing God complete freedom in our worship services. The freedom we give God allows Him to move and bring us into unprecedented levels of interaction with His Kingdom.

Worship truly moves the heart of God and
His heart moves His hand.

The Intimate Touch of an Infinite God

Michael & Angela Pinkston

CHAPTER FIVE

Infinite and intimate… awestruck wonder and passionate devotion – these concepts seem to be extreme opposites. How can they possibly go together? However, you might say the same about the synthesis of divine nature and humanity of Jesus Christ, or the sovereignty of God and the free will of man. We are convinced that *true worship* requires both intimacy and awe. We must know the awesome, holy, righteous God whose fearsome presence makes us dive for cover, as well as the intimate and grace-filled, loving relationship between the Bridegroom King and His Bride.

MICHAEL

In the early '90s, both Angela and I began connecting with corporate worship and the presence of God for the first time. Many of us called this season "The Renewal." God was doing something fresh and new and we were right in the middle of it. However, we did not know that God was also pouring out His Spirit in many other places. Living in Alaska, before websites and podcasts, we could not know what was going on in Toronto, Holy Trinity Brompton, or with the ministries of Randy Clark and Rodney Howard Browne. All we knew was that every time we came together to worship, the Lord's presence would manifest in ways we had never before seen. Whether it was an outpouring of joy and laughter, massive corporate deliverance, supernatural physical manifestations like glory clouds, angels singing, or oil flowing from someone's hands, it was always a wild and exciting time.

One of the things that captivated me was the worship songs coming out of the Vineyard movement. *Draw Me Close to You* by Kelly Carpenter, *In the Secret* by Andy Park, and *True Love* by David Ruis completely changed my life. The theology presented through these lyrics, along with the manifest presence of God, taught me a way of relating to the Lord that was much deeper than anything I had ever known – I was hooked.

When I began leading worship in 1994, those kinds of songs were the ones I wanted to sing. (I must have led *Holy and Anointed One* 300 times those first years.) I did not allow anything to affect me: the facts that I could not play my guitar well, the youth group did not want to worship to my music, my band was leaving me, and the youth pastor wanted more praise songs. I was loving Jesus, but somehow my worship had become extremely introspective and all about me. Phrases like, "I want," or "I need," filled my worship songs. There was a lack of reverence in my relationship with God and He became small in my eyes. At some point, a friend and mentor of ours asked us a very simple question, "Where are the songs that make God big – the ones that focus on His greatness, His

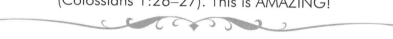

The mystery, hidden for ages and from generations, is now being revealed ... Christ in you, the hope of glory (Colossians 1:26–27). This is AMAZING!

power, and His holiness?" At that point, we did not know, but they certainly were not prevalent in our repertoire!

It is a hard thing to believe that God can do the impossible if we only see Him as touchable. We can reduce the presence of the Holy Spirit to the feeling of a hug as we remind ourselves that He will never leave or forsake us. Intimacy with God should by no means lessen His majesty. Rather, His overwhelming magnificence can be the very thing that catapults us into spiritual ecstasies. To recognize how big, how great, and how powerful God is only makes His nearness all the more special.

The mystery, hidden for ages and from generations, is now being revealed ... Christ in you, the hope of glory (see Colossians 1:26–27). This is AMAZING! Yet, surprisingly, we can sit in church and be bored. When God is small in our eyes, we think nothing of sipping our coffee, checking our smartphones, and chatting with friends during corporate worship times. There is nothing like a revelation of God in His glory to get rid of the boredom, and He is more than willing to do this very thing for us.

ANGELA

A number of years ago, I was in Europe on a short-term mission trip when I had the opportunity to visit some of the world's greatest cathedrals. These structural masterpieces pointed to the grandeur of God. I remember the feeling of being in an open space even though I was inside a building. The ceilings were high, the rooms were long, and the artwork was priceless and stunning. Everything pointed to our great God, high and lifted up, a Person far beyond human measure.

My senses were heightened and everything compelled me to "look up" and focus on a God located far beyond the human plane. It was amazing, to say the least. The majesty of God was expressed in those cathedrals in a way I had never been exposed to during my American, Pentecostal upbringing. This new view, or revelation, of God caused a response of worship to well up within me – I could not help myself! Yet, within that awesome majesty, there was no friendship. Stained glass windows told Bible stories of God interacting with men long ago; shrines and icons were scattered throughout, people were bustling about on their tours... but the connection to God seemed distant. When I recognized that every inch of that magnificent structure shouted out that God was unapproachable, I stood in sorrow.

I learned something that day while standing in the middle of that cathedral with grief gripping my heart: awe of God without an awareness of His passionate presence and intimate love causes strife in men. When God is perceived as awe-inspiring but unapproachable, then we must do things to get Him to notice us. Grace is quickly forgotten and works become the way to His favor.

What then? Where is the balance? THERE IS NO BALANCE! We must have both awe and intimacy, each working at 100% in worship. The Greek word *proskyneō*, usually translated "worship" in the New Testament, perfectly defines this condition. It literally means "to bow and to kiss." This begins to describe how seemingly opposite sides of worship can come together. When we activate both bowing and kissing simultaneously, it creates in us what God is seeking (see John 4:23–24).

The "bow" points to the reverential awe, fearsomeness, and majesty of the infinite God. As we focus on and proclaim His greatness, several things begin to happen. Our lives with all their problems and complexities are deflated to their proper size in light of His greatness. We often fail to encounter God because we seek a small, trivial god whom we can manage and control. A god we carry in our back pocket, whose only concern is whatever personal crises we may be having that day. We are not looking for the King of Kings and Lord of Lords — a God who might rattle us to our core, turn our lives upside down and call us to become a new creation who prepares the world for His return.

Another outcome of focusing on and proclaiming the greatness of God is a stirring of our faith that rises up to push out unbelief. It is difficult to continue thinking that a situation is impossible when beholding the glory of God!

Although a part of our problem is being unaffected by God's majestic presence, equally disastrous is forgetting the language of intimacy with God. The "kiss" of *proskyneō* means just that — the passionate love relationship we have with our Bridegroom, Jesus. He desires for us to know His great affection toward mankind in general and to us in particular. He wants us to have the freedom to express our love and devotion to Him in return.

The Greek word proskyneo, usually translated "worship" in the New Testament, literally means "to bow and to kiss." When we activate both bowing and kissing simultaneously, it creates in us what God is seeking (John 4:23–24).

MICHAEL

If you spend time with me, you will quickly learn that I love my wife – a LOT! You will notice this in many different ways: what I say, how I respond when she is in the room, how I spend my time and money, where I go, and what I do. My relationship with Angela directly influences all the various aspects of my life. My love is not merely an idea or a mental aspiration – I express my love in almost everything I do. This is the kind of relationship Jesus wants with us. Our love for Him should be more than a thought or concept. True love affects all that we *are* and all we *do*. In fact, we have to question whether "unexpressed love" is actually love at all.

We may know how to talk about God, perhaps even send Him requests now and then, but many of us have become inadequate in communicating with Him. We may limit this relationship to a time and a place – often only a couple of hours on Sunday and a few moments throughout the week –boxing God and ourselves into *a thing we do* instead of *a relationship we live out*.

THREE WAYS TO GROW IN AWE AND INTIMACY

The most important thing we have learned over the past 17 years of leading worship is that you can always grow in your expression of love and adoration to the Lord. If you feel inadequate in your intimacy with Jesus or flawed in your fascination with His majesty, here are three exercises that will help you.

Ask – It may seem simple, but sometimes we lack what we want merely because we fail to ask for it.

(Angela) Our kids do this sometimes. They will come where we are and perhaps let out a little sigh to let us know they are present and have something on their minds. Then they will ask for

Our love for Jesus should be more than a thought
or concept. True love affects all that we are and
all we do. In fact, we have to question whether
"unexpressed love" is actually love at all!

something they want, but other times they leave the room without even asking! When they fail to ask they never get what they were after. Because we really, really love to bless our children, we may coax the question out of them, but at other times we wait to see what they will do. I am always hoping they will ask, even if I cannot or will not give them what they want. I love to know what is on their heart – what they are thinking and desiring. Nothing melts my heart quicker than knowing my children want to be with me. How much more does our Heavenly Father want us to ask for intimacy with Him? "He who did not spare His own Son, but delivered Him up for us all, how shall He not with Him also freely give us all things?" (Romans 8:32 NKJV). Remember to ask!

Meditate – Meditation is not reserved exclusively for Eastern religions. However, unlike those religions, instead of emptying our mind, we fill it with God's truth. The Bible teaches in the first Psalm that we will be blessed when we continually meditate on the law (God's Word). David made the "testimonies" of the Lord his meditation (see Psalm 119:99). The word translated *meditation* in Psalm 1 literally means to "say a thing repeatedly." This suggests consciously setting your mind on a matter by talking about it to yourself. Which prompts the questions: What is filling your mind? Where do your thoughts go when they wander? That is usually the problem – our minds wander.

Revelation often comes on the heels of meditation. When you receive a revelation, do not just keep it inside – speak it out to glean from it, and write it down to remember it.

Try meditating on the hymns found in the book of Revelation (for example: Revelation 4:8–11 and 5:9–10). These Scriptures are great descriptions of the majesty of God. To explore intimacy with God, read and meditate on Scriptures in the Song of Solomon and the Psalms. When you begin filling your mind with the majesty of Jesus and God's great love for you, the eyes of your understanding will soon be enlightened.

Carry – Take all of the revelation you receive from God into your next worship time, whether personal or corporate. Thank God for revealing Himself to you and offer up praise for this new understanding. Worship Him. Be amazed. Be undone by His affections and then… do it all over again.

God is seeking those who will worship Him in spirit and in truth. Let us give Him what He desires. Let us honor and adore Him. It is the least we can do for our infinite and intimate God. In some wonderful and mysterious way, a simple physical action in worship can have greater implications in the spiritual dimension than we can possibly imagine.

LECTIO DIVINA:
A NEW (ANCIENT) WAY OF EXPERIENCING GOD

STEVE MITCHELL

CHAPTER SIX

Lectio Divina may be new to you but, in fact, it is an ancient way of divine communication. This simple, very practical method is a means anyone can use to have a two-way conversation with God and remain centered in truth. Most of all, however, it is a way to experience God in a very true sense. This method of divine communion is called "Lectio Divina" (pronounced lex-ee-oh di-vee-nuh). Although people have used it for more than 1,500 years, most of us have never heard of it.

Lectio Divina is a Latin phrase that can be translated "divine reading." Many early monks and holy men approached God by this means. This is how they did it:

- During a time set aside for prayer, the monk went to a private place and began to read aloud a passage of Scripture.

- The monk repeated it audibly until a particular word or phrase stood out to him.

- Then he would stop and ponder it, considering it a word from God for him. This led naturally into prayer as the monk offered back to God what he heard. He'd move deeper into prayer, finally coming to rest in the presence of God.

If you would like to try this method, let me suggest beginning with a simple, easily understood passage of Scripture. If you do not know which one to use, try Matthew 11:28-30. Read it audibly in the manner described previously, just as the early monks did. Keep in mind: spiritual reading is not just racing through the Bible to complete it in a year, so there is no need to cover a given amount of text. Simply read and re-read until you sense God's presence.

Pope Benedict XVI, the current head of the Catholic Church, stated: "I would like in particular to recall and recommend the ancient tradition of Lectio Divina: the diligent reading of Sacred Scripture accompanied by prayer brings about that intimate dialogue in which the person reading hears God who is speaking, and in praying, responds to Him with trusting openness of heart. If it is effectively promoted, this practice will bring to the Church—I am convinced of it—a new spiritual springtime."

LEARN FROM THE ANCIENTS

Since the earliest times, it was common to read aloud. In his autobiographical work, *The Confessions of St. Augustine* written about 398 AD, this bishop reminisced about how he'd marveled

Historical evidence suggests that silent or inaudible reading did not become common until the 10th century. What can we learn from this information? For one thing, when the Bible was written, it was intended to be read aloud.

at the way Ambrose, bishop of Milan, read Scripture: "His eyes traveled across the pages and his heart searched out the meaning, but his voice and tongue stayed still." Augustine's offhand comment shows us that *silent reading*, in His day, was out of the ordinary.

Augustine's description of Ambrose's silent reading happens to be the first definite instance of such a method of reading recorded in Western literature. Other evidence abounds that ancient civilizations, including the Hebrews, practiced *audible reading*.

The Bible certainly corroborates this in Acts chapter 8. Philip, the evangelist, was on the road toward Gaza, and "met the treasurer of Ethiopia, a eunuch of great authority under the Kandake, the queen of Ethiopia. The eunuch had gone to Jerusalem to worship, and he was now returning. Seated in his carriage, he was *reading aloud* from the book of the prophet Isaiah" (Acts 8:27–28 NLT, emphasis added).

Historical evidence suggests that silent or inaudible reading did not become common until the 10th century. (Some evidence indicates that it was even much later than that.) What can we learn from this information? For one thing, when the Bible was written, it was intended to be read aloud. In fact, until well into the Middle Ages, writers assumed their readers would hear, as opposed to see, the text.

Public Scripture Readings

Public, audible reading in the days of antiquity was common. The main reason for this may have been that illiteracy was nearly universal.

Church gatherings were no exception. This understanding sheds more light on why Paul exhorted the church of Thessalonica:

> I charge [adjure, solemnly implore] ... that this epistle be read to all the holy brethren (1 Thessalonians 5:27 NKJV).

> Now when this epistle is read among you, see that it is read also in the church of the Laodiceans, and that you likewise read the epistle from Laodicea (Colossians 4:16 NKJV).

> Blessed is he who reads and *those who hear* the words of this prophecy" (Revelation 1:3 NKJV, emphasis added).

There are many other examples in the Bible supporting the practice of the audible reading of Scripture; instances can be found in both Old and New Testaments. Jesus Himself practiced reading aloud, as recorded in Luke 4:16–19.

Could Origin Determine Destiny?

For a number of years there has been a widespread interest among many church members to learn more about the heritage

There are many examples in the Bible supporting the practice of the audible reading of Scripture; instances can be found in both Old and New Testaments. Jesus Himself practiced reading aloud, as recorded in Luke 4:16–19.

and ancestry of the Church. This is due to a desire to find out how the early church functioned and learn what made them such a vibrant, world-changing entity. Many are asking, "What patterns did they follow that we no longer practice?"

Can rediscovering our spiritual DNA reignite our destiny? That curiosity inspired the thoughts found in this chapter. Could audible reading of Scripture, in private and public, be part of the puzzle?

A dramatic early church example of a corporate prayer, which included the audible reading of Scripture, is found in Acts 4:24–31. This group of early believers included a passage from Psalm chapter two in their prayer. This particular example of reading Scripture aloud, coupled with prayer, resulted in an immediate earthquake and dramatic, supernatural results on the streets of Jerusalem.

MY PERSONAL EXPERIENCE

Very often, during a worship gathering I feel drawn to a certain passage of Scripture and read it aloud so everyone can hear. Often these Scriptures describe an epiphany or "open heaven" experience. There are a number of them: Ezekiel 1, Isaiah 6, and Daniel 7 are just a few. However, the one I am most often drawn to is found in Revelation 4 and 5. Sometimes I read an entire chapter aloud, other times only a portion of it. The audible reading of these verses always seems to bridge the gap between space-time and eternity. Reading about an epiphany from the Scriptures seems to bring anticipation for an epiphany in the meeting.

I do not understand the mechanics of it, but I do know Paul wrote to Timothy, "All Scripture is given by inspiration of God" (2 Timothy 3:16 NKJV). The expression "given by inspiration of

God" is a translation of the Greek word *theopneustos*, which simply means "God-breathed." When we read "God-breathed" words audibly, they seem to create a greater awareness of the spirit realm around us.

As a side note, those in the church who like to sing should practice singing the Scriptures. It should be encouraged and done whenever and wherever appropriate.

SPIRITUAL HUNGER

Some may struggle with where to begin reading aloud in the Bible. Think of the Bible as a menu. If we are hungry and go to a restaurant, we scan the menu and order something that we crave at that moment. It works similarly with spiritual food – we scan the Bible for passages that will satisfy our craving.

Numerous Bible verses depict God's Word as something to taste. For example, in Psalm 119:103: "How sweet are Your words to my taste, Sweeter than honey to my mouth!" (NKJV).

There is also no shortage of passages demonstrating God's desire to feed us. In Matthew 15:32 we read, "Now Jesus called His disciples to Himself and said, 'I have compassion on the multitude, because they have now continued with Me three days and have nothing to eat. And I do not want to send them away hungry, lest they faint on the way'" (NKJV). Then He fed the crowd of 4,000 men, plus women and children.

How can Jesus possibly convey this sentiment any stronger than by calling Himself "the bread of life"? Jesus, who is "the Word made flesh," invites "whomsoever" to eat His flesh (see John 6:34–36, John 1:14).

God hardwired us with a spiritual hunger. St Augustine put it this way: "You have made us for yourself, O God, and our hearts are restless until they rest in you." The ancient practice of Lectio Divina is a method proven throughout centuries to satisfy our hunger for deep fellowship with God.

Is Your Lamp Full?

Sandy Lockhart

CHAPTER SEVEN

It is very common for me to wake up to the words, "Mommy, I'm hungry!" My five-year-old is growing. So every morning she wakes up hungry and I immediately make her breakfast. However, her appetite is only temporarily satisfied; food is never far from her mind.

Blessed are those who hunger and thirst for righteousness, for they will be filled (Matthew 5:6 NIV).

As I thought about the way my daughter awakens hungry every morning, and how she is distracted all day long by a need to eat, I asked myself, am I as hungry for God? Am I feeding my spirit all day with the Word, the presence of God, worshipping, and praying without ceasing? Is my life centered on Him and saturated with Him all day and night? Do I go to sleep meditating on Him, dream

A lifestyle of worship begins with living a life of intimacy with the Maker of heaven and earth.

His dreams and wake in the morning hungry to be with Him? Is my heart full all day and my spirit in an attitude of worship before the one true God?

A lifestyle of worship begins with living a life of intimacy with the Maker of heaven and earth.

Are You Keeping Watch?

We are the most prepared for any circumstance life throws at us when God is at the focus of our life and everything is centered around Him. One of the most important things we can do as worshippers is have hearts that are alive, awake, alert, and prepared for the Lord at all times. God is after every part of our lives – all of us. He wants us to operate as priests, ministering *to* Him and ministering *with* Him, just as we will do forever in eternity. We have the privilege of learning to dwell in His house all the days of our lives on earth before going home to be with Him.

Scripture gives us very clear guidelines regarding how to live our lives and position our hearts so He will be honored. One of my favorite life passages is Matthew 25:1–13, the parable of the Ten Virgins:

> At that time the kingdom of heaven will be like ten virgins who took their lamps and went out to meet the bridegroom. Five of them were foolish and five were wise. The foolish ones took their lamps but did not take any oil with them. The wise, however, took oil in jars along with their

lamps. The bridegroom was a long time in coming, and they all became drowsy and fell asleep.

At midnight the cry rang out: "Here's the bridegroom! Come out to meet him!"

Then all the virgins woke up and trimmed their lamps. The foolish ones said to the wise, "Give us some of your oil; our lamps are going out."

"No," they replied, "there many not be enough for both us and you. Instead, go to those who sell oil and buy some for yourselves." But while they were on their way to buy the oil, the bridegroom arrived.

The virgins who were ready went in with him to the wedding banquet. And the door was shut. Later the others also came. "Sir! Sir!" they said. "Open the door for us!" But he replied, "I tell you the truth, I don't know you." Therefore keep watch, because you do not know the day or the hour" (Matthew 25:1–13 NIV).

Wake Up, Sleeper!

A few months ago, the Lord began speaking to me about "keeping watch" and not allowing my spirit to go to sleep. He had been challenging me to live each day in His presence and not allow my everyday life to take priority. He was making me aware that our time is short, this is the hour to pursue His presence, and the time to practice a life of worship is now!

One night I went to sleep completely wrapped up in my own thoughts and concerns, and peace was very far from my heart. A few hours later, the ringing of the phone shocked me out of sleep. I answered, but I could not seem to wake up. The young girl on the phone was obviously intoxicated and called me as a prank. Al-though her speech was riddled with vulgarities, I responded with compassion. However, I could not wake up enough to hear the Lord in that moment and focus on what He might want to say to her. We spoke a few minutes before she hung up, but the entire time I was groggy and unable to hear clearly what the Spirit was saying. I was broken and repentant before the Lord for the rest of the night, because I had been unable to wake up and be "present" when this precious girl called. I was aware that this was a "wake up" call in more ways than one – I had not been keeping watch.

Even Jesus' disciples fell asleep at one of the most critical times of His life:

> Then he said to them, "My soul is overwhelmed with sorrow to the point of death. Stay here and keep watch with me." Going a little farther, he fell with his face to the ground and prayed, "My Father, if it is possible, may this cup be taken from me. Yet not as I will, but as you will." Then he returned to his disciples and found them sleeping. "Could you men not keep watch with me for one hour?" (Matthew 26:38–41 NIV).

AWAKEN MY HEART

I began reading Scriptures about waking yourself, being alert, living in the presence of God and in a place of worship.

> The fire must be kept burning on the altar continuously; it must not go out (Leviticus 6:13 NIV). *God starts the fire but we must feed it and fan it into flame.*

> But you, dear friends, build *yourselves up* in your most holy faith and pray in the Holy Spirit (Jude 1:20 NIV, emphasis mine).

Instead, be filled with the Spirit. Speak to one another with psalms, hymns and spiritual songs. Sing and make *music in your heart* to the Lord, *always* giving thanks to God the Father for everything, in the name of our Lord Jesus Christ (Ephesians 5:18–20 NIV).

For this reason I remind you to *fan into flame the gift of God*, which is in you through the laying on of my hands. For God did not give us a spirit of timidity, but a spirit of power, of love and of self-discipline (2 Timothy 1:6–7 NIV).

I slept but my heart was awake. Listen! My beloved is knocking: "Open to me, my sister, my darling, my dove, my flawless one. My head is drenched with dew, my hair with the dampness of the night" (Song of Solomon 5:2 NIV).

Ways to Wakefulness

What will get us ready to meet the Bridegroom? KNOWING that He is coming, and the time is soon. What can we do to fill our lamps with oil? How can we prepare for His return and live with eager anticipation of the day we hear the trumpet sound? How can we increase our hunger for Him, for His presence, for the things of the Spirit, and for reaching the lost? How can we attain the life of worship to which we are called and for which we were created?

The oil in the virgins' lamps speaks of fuel. So we must ask ourselves: What things are we filling our lives with daily that sustain us and strengthen us to do what we have been created to do? What keeps the fire in our hearts alive and burning, what keeps us lit up and makes us a bright light in a dark world?

What things are we filling our lives with daily that sustain us and strengthen us to do what we have been created to do? What keeps the fire in our hearts alive and burning? What keeps us lit up and makes us a bright light in a dark world?

THE ANSWER: We become saturated in God's oil by spending intimate moments with Him – time in:

- His presence

- His Word

- Personal worship

BREATH OF AWAKENING

We must carve out time to spend with Jesus, and make Him the focus of our existence. We can no longer fit Him into *our lives*; rather we must fit into *His life* for us. We must become constantly awake and alert, looking for our next heavenly assignment, always giving Him praise. Just as it is physically impossible to wake up in the morning, take a deep breath and expect one lung full of air to sustain us for the entire day, it is also impossible to be fully alive without spending time throughout the day in God's presence. We cannot live without oxygen, and we cannot be *fully alive* without continually partaking of the presence of God.

Learning to live a life of worship requires resolve and practice, and it looks different for each person. I do not have the luxury of unstructured days where I can sit in His presence for hours. Like most people, I have to be *deliberate* about spending time with Jesus.

I have to make Him my priority or my life will crowd out our time together. Some days, I am able to set my alarm early and have several uninterrupted hours alone with Him. Other days, I get the day going, then retreat into my room for alone time with Him. Any time is a good time to awaken to the Lord through intimacy with Him:

> Awake, my soul! Awake, harp and lyre! I will awaken the dawn (Psalm 57:8 NIV).

> I rise before dawn and cry for help; I have put my hope in your word (Psalm 119:147 NIV).

The Worship-Driven Life

There is a reason we need to put God first each day: it aligns our day, centers our thoughts and hearts, and fills our lamps with oil for that day. There is a divine order for our lives, and I believe that spending alone time with God each day is crucial to living a life that overflows with worship.

As a worshipper, I have discovered that it is more important to spend time alone with Jesus, meditating on His Word, resting in His love, and dwelling in His presence than any other thing. When I worship Jesus in the morning, my spirit is filled and I find myself worshipping all day long. Whether driving, shopping, parenting, working, or doing chores, I am living in the midst of worship. When living in His presence, my perspective is shifted to gaze upon Him, and I find that His joy becomes my strength:

> Be joyful always; pray continually; give thanks in all circumstances, for this is God's will for you in Christ Jesus (1 Thessalonians 5:16-18 NIV).

There is a reason we need to put God first each day:
it aligns our day, centers our thoughts and hearts, and
fills our lamps with oil for that day.

The Lord is my strength and my shield; my heart trusts in him, and he helps me. My heart leaps for joy, and with my song I praise him (Psalm 28:7 NIV).

Sing for joy to God our strength; shout aloud to the God of Jacob! (Psalm 81:1).

Have Your Being in Him

When I am full from spending time with the Lord, my spirit is alive and it transforms the way I lead worship, the way I write songs, the way I practice my instrument. My preparation to lead worship often comes from times alone with God. I make a list of songs but it is often forgotten in His presence during corporate worship. To be an effective worship leader I do not rely on my gifts, but on my lamp being full, knowing my Lord, and being able to hear His voice. Coming with a full lamp gives me a freedom that takes away the stress and anxiety of leading worship. I can lounge in His love because I know Him and trust where He is leading:

For in him we live and move and have our being. We are his offspring (Acts 17:28 NIV).

The more time you spend in His presence, the hungrier you become for more. You become homesick for heaven. After a time, it becomes difficult to see your life the way you once did, because your heart is changing to be more like His. You no longer sleep the way you once did because your dreams are filled with His dreams. You do not speak the way you used to because you are being consecrated to Him, "Old things have passed away; behold, all things have become new" (2 Corinthians 5:17 NKJV). You do not worship the way you used to because you have a higher revelation of the One you are worshipping. The time comes when your heart aches to be alone with Him and to worship Him.

When you make room in your life for intimacy with Him, drawing near the Lord and allowing Him to come near you, your lamp is filled... you become fully alive... and you awaken to a new world of hope, joy, peace, and love. Your life becomes better, sweeter, more purposeful and more fulfilling than you ever thought possible.

RELEASE
A NEW SONG

JULIE MEYER

CHAPTER EIGHT

Praise the Lord! Sing to the Lord a new song, and His praise in the assembly of saints.

—Psalm 149:1 NKJV—

The word *praise* means "to boast, to celebrate, and to shine forth to the Lord most passionately." When David said, "Praise the Lord," he meant shine forth to the Lord most jealous… for Jealous is His name.

This Psalm is an invitation from King David to everyone to praise the Lord. Praise Him, for He is good. He is kind. He is great and greatly to be praised. Praise Him because He wants all your praise. David goes on to say, "Sing to the Lord a new song," by which he means, sing something new and fresh. Open your mouth and sing from the overflow of your heart because you have seen the goodness of God and encountered His goodness today. Sing to the best of your ability the most beautiful choruses because He is worthy of all your best and He is listening to you.

In Psalm 33:1-3, David writes:

Rejoice in the Lord, O you righteous! For praise from the upright is beautiful. Praise the Lord with the harp; make melody to Him with an instrument of ten strings. Sing to Him a new song; play skillfully with a shout of joy (NKJV).

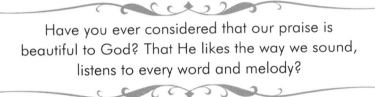

Have you ever considered that our praise is beautiful to God? That He likes the way we sound, listens to every word and melody?

AN AUDIENCE OF ONE

Have you ever considered that our praise is beautiful to God? That He likes the way we sound, listens to every word and melody? During a simple time of singing and genuine worship, the God of the entire universe is our fascinated audience.

Nothing goes unnoticed nor does He forget; the Lord carries every word we utter in worship in His heart. King David always encouraged everyone to sing, to play his or her instruments, and as he wrote repeatedly, to sing a new song. Then he added, "play skillfully." There is something amazing about a truly gifted musician. One who knows how to bend the tones of his instrument to enhance the music. David wanted everything given to God to be excellent.

David's Legacy

When I read the story of King David's life, it moves me. He was the sweet psalmist of Israel. It seems that worship and praise were always a part of his life, even at the age of 17 while tending his "few sheep" on the back hills of Bethlehem. Because David was the youngest son, his father gave him the job of caring for sheep, which was one of the most humble jobs anyone could have. However, he did not sit around and sulk because he got the lowest of jobs; instead, he began to sing. He began to know his God through His instrument and his songs. On those hills of Bethlehem, David began to lift His voice in song to God. Probably there was no one near enough to hear him except the sheep, but that did not stop David, because he was not singing for others – his audience was the Lord.

He wrote down what he sang and thousands of years later, we are still blessed by singing his songs. Can you imagine writing songs that people of every nation will sing thousands of years after you step into eternity?

David sang when no one was listening or watching and in this place of privacy he developed his skills. David wrote and sang about almost everything, and it is all in the book of Psalms. Every aspect of life seemed to move his heart and we know that David moved the heart of God. David was not entirely alone when tending his sheep. The God of all creation was listening to every song of praise, every melody, rhythm, and beat – the God of all creation paid attention to every sound.

Sing Like David Sang

Thoroughout my life, David's heart for God and God's heart for David has moved me. God even called David "a man after His own heart" (1 Samuel 13:14). David studied and understood the emotions of God's heart, and he ran *to* God instead of *away* from Him. David wrote psalms during every season of his life. He went to war with a song on His lips. In the depths of despair, he was singing. In the midst of a storm, He was praising. Whatever the situation in King David's life, he sang from his heart to God. Singing psalms to the Lord was David's way of life.

In 1983, I decided to adopt David's lifestyle and began singing his psalms. I immediately made a wonderful discovery: singing Scripture is the easiest and quickest way to remember it. Since then, I have used this exercise around the world in my Prophetic Singing Workshops.

During my devotional times, I began singing Scripture from the Bible word for word. I would sing it repeatedly until I found a melody that fit with the words. For instance, I sang Psalm 116:1-2:

I love the Lord, because He hears my voice and my supplications. Because He has inclined His ear to me, therefore I shall call upon Him as long as I live.

Sound It, Pray It, Own It

The first time through, I would sing the Scripture exactly the way David wrote it. I would play a couple of simple chords and sing my own melody; whatever came to my mind, I simply sang.

Then, I would take the same Scripture and turn it into a prayer. Still singing and using a couple of chords, or without accompaniment, I began to sing the Scripture around the house. However, I would sing it using my own words, as if it was my prayer:

Lord, I love You. I know You hear my voice. I know, right now, You are listening. You love the song that I sing. You are not too busy to hear this simple cry and song from my heart. I know that even now You are bending down just to hear my song and You love to hear the sound of my voice. So I will pray, I will sing forever.

Then I learned to take the same Scripture and sing it as a prophetic word over my soul. I sing the words as if God were singing it over me. *I love this part!* It teaches you to prophesy in song and sing out God's Word over your soul:

I hear your voice. I hear everything you say. And your voice is so very lovely to Me. And your song I love to hear each time you sing. Let me see your face and let me hear your voice. I created you so very lovely. I created you with sounds and melodies in My heart and I love it when you sing out. I love to hear your songs and every time you sing, I am bending down just to hear every word. Not one word is unnoticed or unheard. So sing again and sing aloud. Let Me hear a fresh new sound, for I love the way I made you. You are Mine and I am yours.

Every day, I have a song in my heart while I am cleaning, cooking, or whatever. I am singing God's Word while folding clothes or driving. If, like David, you will sing when no one is around and will fill your heart with song, then when you are in public your worship will merely be an overflow of what you have experienced all week long.

LEARN GOD'S HEART

In England a couple of years ago, I was teaching on The Prophetic Song at a workshop on prophetic singing. We were doing this very exercise and using this same Scripture. After the workshop, an 86-year-old man came up with tears running down his cheeks. He said, "I have never done that before, singing the Word like that. I thought it was a little funny, but I decided to try it anyway. I was not prepared for how God touched my heart through my simple song."

He went on to say that he had given his life to the Lord many years ago, when he was in his 20s, but always felt like he was a slave in the master's house who could be asked to leave at any time. He said for many years he felt as if he were alone and did not fit in. Then, he told me, "Today, when I began to simply sing this Psalm as a prophecy over my life, I found myself singing, 'Why, I have heard every single word you have ever prayed.'" He said, "Suddenly, I got it. God has been with me all the time. He listened to my voice, and heard every word I said."

This wonderful 86-year-old gentleman ran straight into the love of the Father when he simply began to sing the Word of God and prophesy it over his heart.

This is powerful. Think about it – by singing a simple melody to God's Word, he was changed! As you sing the Word of God, you will encounter God's heart for you, too.

Birth Your David

I want to share an amazing dream. During this dream, I felt as if I was alive in King David's day. I saw his passion to be skilled

Think about it – As you sing the Word of God, you will encounter God's heart for you.

musically and his passion for God's Word. When you mix these two things together equally – you get a David:

In the dream, I was walking beside King David and there was music everywhere. The sounds of stringed instruments filled every room. The music was beautiful and varied, with many different musical themes and scales. There were rehearsal areas where musicians and singers practiced, practiced, and practiced. The training and polishing was non-stop. The sound in the atmosphere was amazing and filled every hall I walked through. I recognized that these men and women, both young and old, had given hours and years to studying their instruments.

However, the singers and musicians were also studying the written Word – the Torah. There were small rooms where they would study the Torah with a teacher. They studied the Law with as much passion as they studied their instruments.

In the dream, King David walked from room to room and became involved, as a mentor, in both their study and practice sessions. Study of the Torah, musical lessons, and practice sessions continued all day long.

Then, King David turned and looked into my eyes and said, "When you have excellence of heart (which I knew referred to the study of God's Word), combined with an excellence of skill – you get a David." He repeated, "When you have excellence of heart combined with excellence of skill – THEN you get (or birth) those who have the skill and heart of David."

God was telling me that He yearns for those who long for His Word and have a beautiful song of praise on their lips. This is who King David was, and God is again raising up young and old singers and musicians for the glory and fame of His Son, Jesus Christ. The whole earth will sing of the glory of the Lord. Then every nation will praise the One who is Worthy.

Sing to the Lord a new song;

Sing to the Lord, all the earth.

Sing to the Lord, praise his name;

Proclaim his salvation day after day.

Declare his glory among the nations,

His marvelous deeds among all peoples.

For great is the Lord and most worthy of praise;

He is to be feared above all gods.

(Psalm 96:1-4 NIV).

PRAISE IS *MOVEMENT*

CALEB BRUNDIDGE

CHAPTER NINE

As a flagger, for me praise is *movement*. A flagger is a person who uses flags while dancing to praise and worship God. I love to flag because it is how God flows through me. It has taken me a while to come to the revelation that God has put people on the earth who like to move when they worship. I call them *praisers* – could you be one?

When I was a child, I was very clumsy and could not dance; I had two left feet and no rhythm. Actually, the enemy had attacked the very area God wanted to use as a spiritual weapon – my freedom of *movement*. Thankfully, I was not detered and entered into the call of God on my life. Don't be hindered by what would seem to be a limitation; even the limitation of a comfort zone! Pick up your weapons of praise and movement. Do not allow anything to render you silent or still!

God is raising up many praisers. I believe these individuals are movers, because the word *praise* implies movement. It is common to hear about intercessors, psalmists, teachers, preachers, prophets, and apostles, but praisers are also a gift to the body of Christ.

Just as our bodies have many parts and each part has a special function, so it is with Christ's body. We are many parts of one body, and we all belong to each other. In his grace, God has given us different gifts for doing certain things well" (Romans 12:4–6 NLT).

TANGIBLE POWER OF PRAISE

Praise is such a powerful gift that God used it to defeat an enemy army attacking Israel:

After consulting the people, the king appointed singers to walk ahead of the army, singing to the Lord and praising him for his holy splendor. This is what they sang: "Give thanks to the Lord; his faithful love endures forever!" At the very moment they began to sing and give praise, the Lord caused the armies of Ammon, Moab, and Mount Seir to start fighting among themselves. The armies of Moab and Ammon turned against their allies from Mount Seir and killed every one of them. After they

It is common to hear about intercessors, psalmists, teachers, preachers, prophets, and apostles, but praisers are also a gift to the body of Christ.

had destroyed the army of Seir, they began attacking each other. So when the army of Judah arrived at the lookout point in the wilderness, all they saw were dead bodies lying on the ground as far as they could see. Not a single one of the enemy had escaped. King Jehoshaphat and his men went out to gather the plunder. They found vast amounts of equipment, clothing, and other valuables – more than they could carry. There was so much plunder that it took them three days just to collect it all! On the fourth day they gathered in the Valley of Blessing, which got its name that day because the people praised and thanked the Lord there (2 Chronicles 20:21–26 NLT).

Praise is so powerful that it brought release to two men in jail:

And at midnight Paul and Silas prayed, and sang praises unto God: and the prisoners heard them. And suddenly there was a great earthquake, so that the foundations of the prison were shaken: and immediately all the doors were opened, and every one's bands were loosed (Acts 16:25–26 KJV).

Praise is so powerful that God called it "His sanctuary." The name *Judah* means, "I will praise the Lord." In Psalm 114:2, the psalmist, speaking of God, said, "Judah [praise] was his sanctuary, and Israel his dominion" (KJV).

PRAISE MEANS MORE THAN YOU THINK

The first mention of praise is the name *Judah,* found in Genesis 29:35:

> Praise is so powerful that God called it "His sanctuary." In Psalm 114:2, the psalmist, speaking of God, said, "Judah [praise] was his sanctuary, and Israel his dominion" (KJV).

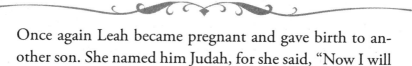

Once again Leah became pregnant and gave birth to another son. She named him Judah, for she said, "Now I will praise the Lord!" And then she stopped having children (NLT).

The next mention of praise is the prophetic blessing Jacob spoke over Judah in Genesis 49:8:

Judah, your brothers will praise you. You will grasp your enemies by the neck. All your relatives will bow before you (NLT).

The English language does not have the depth of meaning required to truly understand the word *praise;* consequently, it fails to express all the ways God expects us to praise Him and the results when we do so. Let's look at the meaning of praise in the Hebrew language. In these definitions, we begin to see the *movement* of praise. They are not the only Hebrew words to describe *movement* in their definition of praise, only a sampling.[1]

YADAH (3034)

To worship with hand extended to the Lord and the giving of oneself in worship and adoration; to lift your hands to the Lord. It means absolute surrender, expressing in movement, "Father, I am all yours, fully submitted to your will alone." It also means to use the hand to toss a stone or arrow and to cast down or throw at or away. This explains how this form of praise affects the enemy.

Genesis 29:35, 2 Chronicles 7:6; 20:21;

Psalm 9:1; 28:7; 33:2; 42:5,11; 49:18; Isaiah 12:1

TEHILLAH (8416)

To sing, to reverence by singing a spontaneous new song to the Lord. Singing aloud a melody in your heart and adding words to it. This special kind of singing can bring tremendous unity to the body of Christ. It is a way of singing directly to God, which is the only praise God will inhabit or be enthroned upon! God manifests Himself in the midst of this exuberant outward and public praise.

Psalm 22:3; 34:1; 40:3; 66:2; 2 Chronicles 20:22

BARAK (1288)

This is to kneel or bow in reverence to God as an act of adoration. It implies continually and consciously giving "place" to God and blessing the Lord by extolling His virtues in adoration. This is to bow or kneel physically as the heart yields to Him and acknowledges Him as your King. When your heart is postured in kneeling and blessing the Lord, then out of the "abundance of your heart" the mouth speaks praise. As you remain focused on the Lord, your praise will hold the enemy and his intentions at bay:

Psalm 34:1; 103:1–5 & 20–22;

1 Chronicles 29:20; Nehemiah 8:6

HALAL (1984)

To be clear (transparent), to shine, to make a show, to boast, to rave, and celebrate; to give light, to make a fool of oneself – to act like a madman. Interestingly this word for exaggerated praise is the root of *hallelujah*! The halal causes a flashing forth of light that implies the banishing of darkness.

1 Chronicles 16:4; 23; 25:3; 29:13; Nehemiah 12:24

TOWDAH (8426)

This to give worship by extending the hand in adoration or agreement with what has been done or will be. It says that something is finished or completed. The right hand symbolizes our covenant with the Father. When God extends His right hand in covenant, He is saying, "All I have is yours" and the corresponding extension of *your* right hand to Him says the same. God honors this sacrifice by performing miracles. This is also a giving of thanks or praise as a sacrifice before the manifestation of a miracle. It is a thanking or praising of God for something not yet evident in the natural. This form of praise rests upon the truth of God's Word and the recognition that a sacrifice with faith is required.

Psalm 42:4; 50:23; Jeremiah 17:26

ZAMAR (2167)

To sing or make music accompanied by instruments. It also means to touch the strings. It refers to praise that includes instrumental worship, hence to celebrate in song or music.

Psalm 92:1; 150:1–6

SHABACH (7623)

To address boisterously a loud adoration such as a shout! Proclaim loudly and unashamed the glory, triumph, power, mercy, and love of God. This word implies that testimony is praise. To shout unto the Lord is an action of shabach. We are to put our whole self into it, totally uninhibited. This praise causes a quieting or stilling of the enemy, as a lion's roars paralyzes its prey.

Psalm 63:3–4; 117:1

CHAGAG (2287)

This is to make a pilgrimage, to keep a pilgrim's feast, celebrate a feast by dancing, reeling, and moving in a circle, to march in a sacred procession to observe a festival; it also implies being giddy.

1 Samuel 30:16–17 NKJV)

CHUWL (2342)

To bear, to dance, drive away, or fall grievously with pain. Chiyl, the root of Chuwl, means to twist or whirl in a circular or spiral manner, specifically to dance, or to writhe in pain especially in childbirth or fear. Figuratively it means to bear, bring forth, dance, and drive away.

Judges 21:23 (NKJV)

KARAR (03769)

This is to whirl, dance whirling, dancing:
Then David *danced* before the Lord with all his might; and David was wearing a linen ephod. So David and all the house of Israel brought up the ark of the Lord with shouting and with the sound of the trumpet (2 Samuel 6:14–15 NKJV, emphasis added).

Seven of the words I've listed are considered the primary words for praise: Yadah, Tehillah, Halal, Towdah, Zamar, Shabach, and

Zamar. The other words for praise, though not as common, are also of great importance. Chuwl, for example, is the only word that says there is *movement* in intercession. Chagag describes the worship of making a feast to God. Karar explains the uninhibited dance of David when bringing the ark of the covenant into Jerusalem.

PRAISE BRINGS RENAISSANCE

Everything in the earth is released to give praise to God: "Praise him, O heaven and earth, the seas and all that move in them" (Psalm 69:34 NLT). However, all creation is waiting for the sons of God to join in bringing praise to the Lord in the age to come. The Message puts it this way:

> I don't think there's any comparison between the present hard times and the coming good times. The created world itself can hardly wait for what's coming next. Everything in creation is being more or less held back. God reins it in until both creation and all the creatures are ready and can be released at the same moment into the glorious times ahead. Meanwhile, the joyful anticipation deepens. All around us we observe a pregnant creation. The difficult times of pain throughout the world are simply birth pangs. But it's not only around us; it's within us. The Spirit of God is arousing us within. We're also feeling the birth pangs. These sterile and barren bodies of ours are yearning for full deliverance. That is why waiting does not diminish us, any more than waiting diminishes a pregnant mother. We are enlarged in the waiting. We, of course, don't see what is enlarging us. But the longer we wait, the larger we become, and the more joyful our expectancy (Romans 8:18–25 MSG).

There is so much movement in this passage! I challenge you to read the Scriptures in this chapter again and again. Allow them to break you out of traditional thinking and make way for the King of Kings to ride into the earth on your praise. Surely, when we all come together and praise Him in unity, the King will make His triumphal return to earth.

---

[1]The number following each Hebrew word is its index number in *Strong's Exhaustive Concordance of the Bible* and the descriptions are the author's paraphrase of definitions.

TOUCHED BY WORSHIP

A LITTLE BOY'S STORY

ART LUCIER

CHAPTER TEN

I am confident you have received fresh insight already about worship and the power of praise. Though it would be much easier for me to unlock for you some Scriptures about worship or the tabernacle of David and praise, I feel the leading of the Lord to share a couple of stories and thoughts on what can happen when worship touches a child, all from my personal life.

SET APART

Before I tell my story, just to keep things legitimate, I want to share a favorite Scripture on worship that is relevant to my story. You will find it in Acts 13:1–2:

> In the church at Antioch there were prophets and teachers: Barnabas, Simeon called Niger, Lucius of Cyrene, Manaen

(who had been brought up with Herod the tetrarch) and Saul. While they were *worshipping* the Lord and fasting, the Holy Spirit said, "*Set apart* for me Barnabas and Saul for the work to which I have called them" (NIV, emphasis added).

Set apart – what a powerful statement and commissioning of Barnabas and Saul! Notice where and when this happened – it was during a worship service! I have seen more transformation happen in peoples' lives during one hour of worship than from months of reaching out and preaching to them. You may have noticed that worship often stimulates the prophetic and this account of commissioning would make it seem that has always been the case.

Does God "set apart" people for His purposes? Let me tell you how the Lord used a worship service in a small Catholic church in a little Canadian town to set apart a young child for His purposes.

HE TOUCHED ME

Easter Sunday, 1973, I was four years old, or would be the next day. I have a better memory than most but what would happen to me this day would be impossible for anyone to forget. Our old Catholic church was of classic design – complete with a steeple, a balcony, and creaky wood flooring. Even then, it was showing its age; in only a few years, the city would tear down this landmark to make room for a mall. That was in the future, but today the choir was declaring the resurrection of the King of Kings, and more people were filling the pews than usual. Since my mother was in the choir, I could sit anywhere I wanted.

My father was not with us; He was at home as usual. He was not much of a "churchgoer" back then, so it was just mom and me. I headed up to the balcony, the favorite place of most kids my age. There was something about the bird's-eye view that many of us liked, and the front of the balcony had an excellent view for a little guy like me.

Although I do not recall my mother singing in the choir before, I do remember her singing with the faithful that day. Mom would prefer that I not sit in the balcony, but she had to remain with the choir during the entire service. Consequently, I had the freedom to take my elevated seat with its panoramic view.

Even though I do not remember much of the service, I do remember loving the music and hearing the collective voices of the choir. I was not able to read a hymnal yet, and there was no projection of the words on a screen, but I did my best to join in the singing. I shall never forget one particular hymn we sang to HIM on that day: "Holy, Holy, Holy, Lord God Almighty, Early in the morning our song shall rise to Thee."

"Holy, Holy, Holy, Lord God Almighty, Early in the morning our song shall rise to Thee."

During that song, IT hit me! I should maybe say, He touched me – not on the outside – but inside. I was deeply moved by the presence of the Holy Spirit deep within and I began sobbing.

The presence of God touched me powerfully and I remember trying to figure out what was happening and trying to make sense of my experience. Was the power in the music?

I remember thinking that the music possibly released something. As a child, I had no understanding of spiritual things, no answers, no way to evaluate what had happened. But a day would come that I would discover I did not need any.

A CHILD'S PASSION FOR THE WORD

One year and one day later, an excited young boy got a birthday gift from his mother that he will never forget. Not only would I not forget that gift, it is the only one I remember – I do not remember any birthday gifts I received before that one or afterward. What could so totally grab the attention of a five-year-old boy? It was a children's Bible, with pictures! I read and re-read that book until the pages fell out. I still recall the pictures of Moses and the Red Sea parting, Samson killing a lion with his bare hands, and Absalom hanging in a tree by his hair. Yet, the excitement did not stop with this little picture Bible; I had a hunger for the stories and things of God that I would soon take with me to school.

A little more than a year later, my mother enrolled me in the Catholic Elementary School. I loved the fact that it was only a block away from home. However, I would soon discover that there was something I would love more than its location. This school had many picture books! Even more than that, the books were about religion and filled with God stories!

The library class was almost as much fun for me as recess. They dismissed us to go to the library to spend 30 minutes finding and reading a book. While my friends were disputing who would get the best dinosaur books, I had no competition checking out and reading Bible story books. I read and re-read the stories of Adam in the garden, Noah and the big boat, Abraham's sacrifice of Isaac. I was in heaven; I loved those stories and remembered each one.

Everyone knew of my love for Bible stories. I found that a good way to let people know what I had learned was in Catechism class. Once a week for one hour, they taught us aspects of the church and things of God, often using Bible stories. At the end of the

What could so totally grab the attention of a five-year-old
boy? It was a children's Bible, with pictures! I read and
re-read that book until the pages fell out. I still recall the
pictures of Moses and the Red Sea parting, Samson killing a
lion with his bare hands, and Absalom hanging in a tree by
his hair.

class, they would question us about what they had just taught. The
teacher asked us to raise our hands if we knew the answer, and my
hand was always in the air. It came to the point where the teacher
would say, "Can someone besides Art tell me about... ?"

I did not win many awards during elementary school, except
for one: the Religious Award. I won that award all seven years I attended that school.

From Altar Boy to Drug Dealer

When I grew older, I served the priest as an altar boy for several
years. I was one of two boys asked to travel with the priest on his
journey to serve various parishes throughout British Columbia. At
this time, I had serious aspirations of one day becoming a priest.

We lived in northern British Columbia, a 15-hour drive from
any major Canadian cities. When I was 12 and heard that the Pope
would be visiting Alberta, the province next to us, I begged my
parents to put me on a bus to go and see him. I wept when they
would not let me go.

Despite attending church Sunday after Sunday and serving as
an altar boy until I was 17, high school was a negative experience
for me. By tenth grade, I was drinking and doing drugs. Because

my family was dysfunctional, I clung to a new group of friends, doing what they did to earn their approval. Unfortunately, I had chosen friends that were even more dysfunctional than my family. Within a year, my school and my parent tossed me out. I began selling drugs to make a living and had my first serious girlfriend, who was only 16 years old.

We had a daughter together when I was 18, but gave her up for adoption because her mom was still only 16. Eighteen months later, in a drug deal gone wrong, my girlfriend was murdered. The authorities found her body in the early hours of November 11, Remembrance Day. World War I ended on this date and it is the day Canadians honor those who died while serving their country.

Because I was not with my girlfriend the night she died, I did not know who she had been with or have any idea who committed this crime; neither did the authorities. I was a suspect in her murder for the five months it took the police to catch her killer.

Beyond Stories, to Experience

During this traumatic time, I sent out a prayer. Even though I was far from Him, I still believed and needed to hear from the God of my childhood. I remembered the stories of God becoming involved with peoples' lives, but now I needed my own experience with Him. And it was coming – God had heard my prayer.

Within two weeks, I found myself at a Pentecostal youth conference a couple of hours from my hometown, where I answered

Now I needed my own experience with Him. And it was coming – God had heard my prayer.

the call to accept Jesus as my Savior. I knew that I desperately needed God, and when I walked to the front during the altar call, God hit me right between the eyes. Instantly, I began prophesying and speaking in tongues at the top of my voice.

When I returned home, I began reading the Bible. I was so hungry for more of God that I read the New Testament once a month for an entire year – God transformed my whole life. I joined the youth group that grew in two months from 20 to 80 youth. I was preaching to everyone: my old friends, people uptown and on the street. I told all about Jesus, who had forgiven and changed me!

It was at this time that I picked up a guitar and began to teach myself how to play and sing. Within six months, I was leading worship and preaching in our local church of 250 – my fire was back!

The feelings I had as a four-year-old boy, I rediscovered! God touched me again and I have never lost it. Although I have made some mistakes during my walk with God over the last 22 years, God has been faithful to lead me into sanctification and change. In addition, He gave me the perfect wife to walk through it with me.

Unlike me, my wife grew up in a Christian, Bible-believing family. She never rebelled but went to Bible college to get her music degree. She has walked with me through thick and thin for 20 years. She has been a tremendous partner in the church we planted eight years ago. My wife is an incredible preacher and worship leader, capable of leading worship with either a guitar or keyboard, and is a good drummer and bass player. Did I mention she also plays flute? She has been a major contributor on both our worship CDs, and she is a gifted songwriter. God was very good to me!

DÉJÀ VU

My wife and I have led worship in Kansas City, Africa, Brazil, and all across Canada, and we know this is only the beginning.

Some of the most exuberant worshippers we encounter are children; they remind me how God touched me as a small child! Ninety percent of the people on our dance floor at church are children. In addition, God blessed me with children who are becoming part of our worship team, and that leads to one final story.

About 10 years ago, our family, along with some young people, drove twelve hours to a Jesus Fest sponsored by Nolan and Heather Clark. It was awesome! Just "Jesus and Blue Sky" was the motto for this five-day outdoor worship festival.

One evening while I was lost in worship, someone came and informed me that my six-year-old son was hurt and crying under the bleachers. I found him sitting on a piece of wood, weeping. I asked him over and over again what had happened but he was crying so hard he could not answer. When he finally calmed down a bit and informed me what had happened, I was shocked! He told me that while we were worshiping on the field, Jesus came to him and asked, "Will you worship ME?" Our son has such a clear memory of this event, he will never forget what happened to him.

I have come to look at the Scripture found in Proverbs 22:6 in a little different light. "Train a child in the way he should go, and when he is old he will not depart from it" (Proverbs 22:6 NIV).

We have to ask ourselves: Are we being the example of a worshipper that our kids will follow? God desires to touch all His children, even the youngest ones. Some may need to reconsider their decision about bringing children to worship events. Psalm 22:3 says that God dwells in the praises of His people. He is waiting to touch people of every age and mark them for Himself. I believe that and know it to be true.

Almost 40 years ago, on the wings of worship in a little old Catholic church, Jesus came, marked me, and set me apart. My prayer is that He would do it again and again to the next generation. "But Jesus said, 'Let the children alone, and do not hinder them from coming to Me; for the kingdom of heaven belongs to such as these'" (Matthew 19:14 NASB).

SIMPLY DEEPER

DENNIS SEE

CHAPTER ELEVEN

There is a line in a song I wrote a few years ago that says, "Here I am once again, wanting to say something not already been said. With all the praise throughout eternity, what can I give to you?" When it comes to worship, it seems as if everything has already been said and done, and there is nothing new and fresh we could possibly give God that He would want to hear. However, that is not true.

He wants to hear from us! He desires our expressions of love and adoration! There are no other beings in creation who can give praise, love, and worship—the song of the redeemed—the way we can (Revelation 5:9). In addition, each of us has a unique sound God longs to hear.

DEEP CALLS TO DEEP

The most profound thing I have learned through my years of serving Him is this: the more we get to know our wonderful God, the more of Himself and His Kingdom He will reveal to us. Psalm 42:7 says: "Deep calls unto deep at the noise of Your waterfalls; All Your waves and billows have gone over me" (NKJV).

This Scripture says to me that there is a deep place in me calling to the deep places in God, and there's a deep place in Him that is calling to me. His voice and thoughts are drenching me, as if I were standing under a waterfall, and His call drowns out the sounds of this world like waves crashing on a beach, making me hungry for more of Him. I hear the roar, power, and beauty in His words pouring over my life, and it makes me want more of Him.

The infinite God we serve is like a diamond with countless facets. He has aspects and attributes we have never seen. It requires eternity to come to know all the facets of God. I have heard it said that one of the reasons the angels continually say, "Holy, Holy, Holy," is because they are always seeing a new side of God. We cannot wrap our minds around this idea because we are so limited.

However, we were created to walk in a heavenly realm of worship. Worship is not just singing songs or part of the "order of service," although it is a form of worship. It is a lifestyle of reverencing and honoring God with all we are and in everything we say and do.

Worship is one of the most incredible tools, awesome pleasures, and powerful secret weapons God has given us. Once we really understand what worship is all about, we need never again walk in defeat. Yes, you can be in a place that is solid and unmoving no matter what happens in your life. Even the most tragic event cannot move you when you learn to walk in a lifestyle of worship.

Worship in the Spirit Realm

When I was a new Christian, God took me into the spirit realm and began to show me worship unlike anything I had ever before witnessed. At first, I was drawn to it because it was unique and more beautiful than anything I had ever heard. I thought I was imagining it, but quickly realized that God was allowing me to hear the worship He likes. Over the next few months, that music kept drawing and calling to me.

Worship is one of the most incredible tools, awesome pleasures, and powerful secret weapons God has given us.

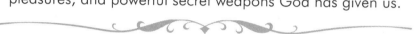

I was raised in a church that sang three hymns and had all the rituals and liturgies that many churches use. I am not criticizing that kind of worship, but it was not enough for me because it did not allow me time for an encounter with God and His Holy Spirit. From an early age, I knew there was something more to worship, but I did not know what it was. As a new Christian, I was thrilled with the changed life I was experiencing, but I wanted more – I wanted a better worship experience.

Soon I was asking God to show me my destiny, what He wanted me to do. I felt I lacked talents and asked God to give me some of His gifts. Music began coming into my heart. Through the Holy Spirit I knew God had called me to sing, write, and play music.

Before I accepted Christ, I led a rebellion in the eighth grade to have music taken out of the public school system, because to me it was a torture to learn it. Little did I know a short while later I would give my life to Jesus and He would call me to a life devoted to worship. God has a sense of humor.

After becoming born again, music attracted me and I began hearing songs inside me. So one day, I sat down at a piano and tried playing what I was feeling and hearing. At first, I could only pick out the melody, but I soon started learning chords and writing down those little songs. I heard both the words and music, writing them down at the same time. Then I poured these songs out to the Lord as an offering. In other words, I was giving myself to the Lord through the music He gave to me. For hours, I would play to the Lord spontaneous songs and whatever was on my heart.

This taught me the importance of worship in my relationship with God. He told me that He would train me and teach me by His Holy Spirit, whom He had given me as a friend and helper. I had never heard of people having conversations with God, and I did not know if I was "authorized" to have these talks with Him.

SNAPSHOTS OF THE FUTURE

Most people I knew did pray and gave God their requests, but no one mentioned that He talked back. I soon realized the "worship thing" I was doing was extremely important; I couldn't understand why other people didn't do it. Almost everyone I knew was satisfied with singing a few songs and praying a couple of prayers. I knew in my heart that God wanted a deeper relationship with all His people so they, too, could connect with Him as I was able to.

During that time, I begged God to show me what He wanted to do with my life. He eventually showed me a vision with thousands of pictures of my future. However, they flashed in front of me so fast that I finally yelled, "Stop, I can't take it." Even though I had been asking for this very thing for many weeks, the snapshots of future events in my life came so fast and furiously they quickly overwhelmed me.

One thing I remember from that vision was seeing a stadium full of people and me leading them in the same type of deep worship I was experiencing. It would begin as just a weekend meeting and then continue for days and even weeks, as thousands of people came from all over the world because of the miracles, signs, wonders, and heavy anointing and presence of God.

What I saw during the vision that may help every believer go into a deeper place of worship is simple sounding yet profound in the doing – we must come to Him as little children with a childlike faith in His goodness. When we ask God for these experiences, we have to be diligent to believe that He will give them to us.

Keys to His Presence

Now I have been leading worship for years, in meetings small and large; but every gathering, to me, is the "most important" one. We may think when only a few people are in attendance the worship is not as important as in a larger meeting, but this is not true.

God's Word says clearly in Matthew 18:20, "For where two or three are gathered together in My name, I am there in the midst of them" (KJV). Therefore, the most important thing is that God is in the meeting. The key to His presence is a meeting that is "in His name."

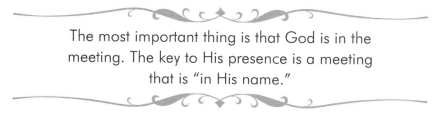

The most important thing is that God is in the meeting. The key to His presence is a meeting that is "in His name."

In addition, we need to come to a deep understanding of some things many of us take for granted – who we are in Him and what

He did for us by going to the Cross. These are simple-sounding yet key elements to going deeper in worship. Once we get a revelation of the authority and power He gave us and learn to use it in worship, look out! We will change the world as we go from glory to glory! (2 Corinthians 3:18)

When you make a place for God, He will come to you, speak to you, and take you places you never imagined. In addition, He will give you the knowledge of when to release the things He shows you. I have often tried to explain things I got from the Lord but they have not made sense because I failed to wait for His timing. I believe He wants to reveal much more to His children but we need to learn when to speak and when to be silent, and to use our born-again spirits rather than depending on our minds to understand "deeper" things.

God wants to show us things to come and give us gifts. However, He must be able to trust us to get all the details right and only share our revelations in His timing. In addition, if we only use revelations to make ourselves look good and appease our insecurities, He will not be able to confide them to us.

God wants to show us things to come and give us gifts.
However, He must be able to trust us to get all the details
right and only share our revelations in His timing.

POSITION YOURSELF TO SIMPLY HEAR HIM

One thing I have learned to do is spend time "waiting on the Lord," not asking for things, or even praying… just listening and waiting. Almost everything I get from God comes through *worship* and *waiting* on the Lord. This is difficult if you are a busy person like me. However, we must fight to stay in that place of "waiting and ministering" to the Lord, because this is the place from which all *real* ministry, anointing, and power comes.

Remember, everything is by faith. Faith is another simple but profound key to going deeper. Hebrews 11:6 says:

> But without faith it is impossible to please Him, for he who comes to God must believe that He is, and that He is a rewarder of those who diligently seek Him (NKJV).

Purity of heart is also a key to seeing God in our worship. Matthew 5:8 says, "Blessed are the pure in heart, For they shall *see God*" (NKJV, emphasis added).

When I worship, I meditate on these Scriptures because God says this is the way to get results, when we would "see" and "seek" Him! What would it be like if we came together with child-like faith, believing His Word is true, and He will *actually* do what it says? We would see God move like never before because we have made ourselves ready for Him.

To go deeper in worship and experience things He wants us to may require throwing aside our traditions, "going for God" with everything in us, and letting the Holy Spirit lead the way. This may sound simple, too good to be true. Some may not be able to hear what I'm saying because they like their own way of doing it and have had some success in worship, but there is so much more waiting for us! Unless God is in our midst by His Holy Spirit, we must question if what we're doing is the kind of worship God desires.

Some may say, "Yah, yah, I know that, but what is the *real* secret to going deeper into realms of worship?" The secret of deep is simply to "wait on the Lord" and then do like Jesus did – perform what you hear or see in the spirit.

Our hearts long to encounter what other people have experienced in worship. We want to see in the spirit and have visions and prophetic words. We want to hear sounds and smell fragrances, and more! Friends, I am telling you it really is this simple: let God soften your heart; get alone with Him, listen and wait.

What follows is a frightening prayer for some, because we must be willing to lay "our own thing" down and become open to new ideas and ways of doing things. The process may be uncomfortable, yet if you will do this, God will take you to a new place in Him and show you *His* ideas of worship.

With a pure heart, ask:

Lord, I want to know You. Please, teach me to know You and show me the worship of heaven. Show me Your heart. I repent for trying to get to You through rituals and formulas. Now I simply come to You asking for Your help. Holy Spirit, please lead me to the Father and show me how to worship in a way that pleases Him. Put Your songs and prayers in me... let me say what You want said... let me hear with Your ears. I give You my heart, Lord. Amen!

THE GOD-DATE

VINCE GIBSON

CHAPTER TWELVE

It seems that, in today's society, the word *mandate* gets thrown around quite a bit. Political figures, from pulpits at home and abroad, lay out their mandates, almost weekly, to change everything from economies to education, or sometimes just to tickle the ears of their constituents. Churches, businesses, movements, and even popular culture, seem to always keep a mandate before their congregations, employees and followers. Mandates provide us with direction and guidance.

What about the mandate of worship leaders, musicians, and worshippers? A few years ago as I was studying, I felt God lay a "God-date" on me, and it has become my life passion in worship. I say "God-date" because the very definition of the word *mandate* seems to imply that they usually come from, you guessed it – man! "God-dates" come from the One whose Word is everlasting.

Mandates seem to flux with the environment of the day, month, or year. I love the Scripture where it says that Jesus Christ is the same yesterday, today, and forever (Hebrews 13:8). He never changes, yet His mercies are new every morning! I say all that because of lessons I've been learning about God-dates in my own life. It seems that just when we begin to get comfortable where God has us and what He has been teaching us, it changes – or does it? God is infinite; don't try to understand because you can't – neither can I. He knows all truth from all the ages past, and none of it has or will ever change in the ages to come. He also knows my human mind, though fearfully and wonderfully made, can only absorb so much. If He were to let me see even a glimpse of the fullness of what He carries, it would simply be too much for this earthly body. Even Isaiah, after seeing God on the throne surrounded by angels, basically said, "I'm as good as dead."

God builds precept upon precept and line upon line; though His truth never changes, He gives us the grace to understand more and more of it. Don't ever come to the place where you're not willing to flex and change everything you thought you knew about Him. He won't contradict Himself, but He will reveal more of Himself to show us His bigger picture.

The God-date begins in the book of Esther. Most of you have probably read the story of Esther and taken away great lessons from someone who was willing to give up everything for God and nation. If you don't know the story, let me refresh you. In short, the king threw a party and decided he wanted to show off his queen. That particular day the queen was apparently in no mood for gawkers. The king called for her; she refused to come. Refusing the king is not the best of ideas, as she soon found out. The king decided she was no longer needed as queen. Talk about a bad day at work!

As with many decisions we make, the kings decision at the time seemed most wise, but he soon realized life without a queen was not exactly what he had bargained for. So what's a king to do? Get another queen! A call went out across the land for the most beautiful virgins to assemble in order to find a new queen – this is where things get interesting. All the women were assembled at the king's palace and placed in the custody of a man named Hegai.

Hegai's whole job was to prepare the virgins for their encounter with the king. He gave them everything they could need before they were called into the king's chamber. His job was to know what the king liked. For one year, Hegai would see to it that the maidens had beauty treatments of myrrh and sweet odors. While reading this, I began to think how hard it must have been for Hegai to not want to take the maidens for himself – but he couldn't. Hegai was a eunuch and unable to produce anything of his own doing; his job was not to please himself – his job was to please the king and prepare the maidens for the moment they would be called away.

Hegai's story began to jump off the page as a type and shadow of what we are called to do – our God-date. We are called, as worshippers, to prepare the Bride for an encounter with the King! Sometimes in the past I've been guilty of getting so caught up in my own pleasure of worship that I forget I'm leading His Bride to an encounter. There is no glory for myself and I should not be reproducing anything that would point to me.

I should be solely focused on the One who has called for His Bride. Every song I sing, every word I say, should be to lead everyone I can to His chamber.

I should be solely focused on the One who has called for His Bride. Every song I sing and every word I speak should be to lead everyone I can to His chamber. I'm not attempting to duplicate my worship experience, I am just a facilitator to bring His Bride right up to the chamber doors of the King.

Sometimes our worship can become spiritual hedonism if we are not careful. It becomes all about filling our own happiness and self pleasures. Don't misunderstand me, some of the greatest moments of my spiritual life have been soaking one-on-one and face-to-face with Christ and in corporate times of worship where it seems as if we are all ascending to the throne together. There are moments when it's just me and Him and it's the greatest pleasure I find living here on this earth. However, I must remember that I am called to be a Hegai! If we are always inner focused and never focused toward those He has called to an encounter, how will we ever be able to break out of our "cloud" and reach them?

As a lead worshipper, it's my job to know what the King is all about and create the atmosphere where His Bride is easily able to walk into His chambers and be changed forever. In fact, once the maidens had gone in to the king, they didn't return to the same house; they went to a different house of women in the palace. This is so amazing – once we have led the Bride to an encounter with the King they will never be the same. Oh, they may have their moments of forgetfulness, but there will always be that moment that sticks with them forever, when they met face-to-face with the King.

As I envision Hegai, I can see him walking Esther up to the door of the king's chamber and the door closing behind her. Hegai walks away with a smile, knowing he has completed the mandate the king asked of him. He is never mentioned again after this. True to his title as a eunuch, he disappears, having produced nothing for himself and bringing no glory to his position and rank.

One second with God will do more with a life than anything humanly possible. Healing, deliverance and forgiveness can all take place in His chambers, but the most important thing that will happen will be the love the Father lavishes upon them. One gaze into His eyes, one touch from his burning heart, and they will never return the same.

Today God is asking us, "What will you put aside of your own desires to reach My Bride and facilitate an encounter with Me?"

Whether it's leading worship, working at your job, or simply living life, you are the conduit of that encounter. You are the catalyst through which the glory (light) flows. Matthew 5:14–16 says that you are the light of the world (a light to everyone you could possibly come into contact with). You are a city set on a hill that cannot be hidden. People don't light a lamp and put it under a basket, but on a stand (that's you and me), where it gives light to ALL in the house. In the same way, let your light shine before others so that they may see your good works and give glory to your Father who is in Heaven. Christ in you is the hope of glory, not just for yourself, but to the world.

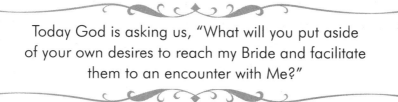

Today God is asking us, "What will you put aside of your own desires to reach my Bride and facilitate them to an encounter with Me?"

Everything gets drawn into the light. Turn on a porch light on a hot summer night and watch the bugs come quickly. People who have near-death experiences often speak about going toward the light. The light has a natural drawing effect. The Light lives in you, and you have the influence of drawing people toward the Light.

There will always be, and should be, moments that it's just you and Him. There should also be moments when your whole purpose is outward focus and your intent is to lead the lost, hurting, and saved to encounter Him. Jesus spent most of His time here on earth in the outer court, not the inner court. He was constantly out with the crowds, leading people to the Father. He came to bring them life... not just life, but life more abundant!

Lastly, there is a great joy that awaits those who weary not in well doing. Hegai's joy came from pleasing the king, not from his own great exploits. Watching people come out of His chambers, changed forever, is all we need to find great joy and strength. Knowing that they have felt the unending love of the everlasting Father is all the satisfaction we need.

I pray a generation like Hegai will arise who will lay down all of themselves to lead people to Christ. God, give them sounds and strategies that would cause them to move people straight into the presence of the Almighty. Show us how to get lower and how to make You higher here upon this earth. Show us how to take folks up the mountain while, at the same time, bringing Heaven down to earth. Help us to make the space between Heaven and earth thin.

24/7 – 365
A GLOBAL WORSHIP
REVOLUTION

SEAN FEUCHT

CHAPTER THIRTEEN

We are living in the days of the most glorious transition ever seen! The worldwide church is transforming into the fullness of its original intention. While the forces of hell rage harder than ever before to cloud the understanding of a generation with oppression, perversion, and darkness, there is a glory rising (see Isaiah 60). There is a fire burning on the worshipping saints that will not be extinguished. This fire, as the prophet remarked in Jeremiah 20:9, is "shut up in [our] bones." This means that it is in our spiritual DNA… it is our mandate – it is our *sound* on the earth.

This worship revolution is not just the latest church-growth fad, slick concert, hot seminar, new charismatic rhetoric, or the catchphrase for a conference brochure. This is the New Testament

Ecclesia, "ruling body" – the church for which Christ died, stepping boldly into its end-time apostolic role of flooding every square inch of earth with the knowledge, revelation, beauty, and glory of God.

Like a torrential flood, it overwhelms everything from typical Sunday morning church services to the darkest nations on the face of the earth! Oh, I can feel the level of worship rising… can you?

27:4 COMES BEFORE 24/7

There is a wildfire of 24/7 worship and prayer in virtually every nation on earth, as God awakens the "heart of David" in His people. This is not a desire to be king, lust for the limelight, or a drive to be seen on a platform. It is the call to intimacy and worship of God. It is a deep well of worship like the one dug by a simple shepherd boy while tending his sheep. It was during his time of lowly service that David cultivated an intimacy that prepared him for the battles, giants, betrayals, and victories to come.

The depth of a generation's intimacy will be the scope of their authority.

The depth of a generation's intimacy will be the scope of their authority. God calls forth a truly apostolic worship movement that will flood the earth with praise, fill the nations with His presence, and establish the dominion of Jesus to invade broken humanity.

This passion and intimacy is birthed in the "secret place" and there are no shortcuts. The reviving of secret places always leads to a reviving in public places!

The establishment of a tabernacle without blood sacrifices was not King David's goal, nor was a religious obligation of 24/7

365-days-a-year worship. Intimacy was his only goal; communion with the Father was his passion. The formation of 24/7 – 365 worship in David's tabernacle was merely an outward manifestation of his inward passion for God. We must remember to continually turn back to our "first love" of cultivating His presence in our lives. The result will be the broadcasting of our affection to the nations!

When I teach in worship schools and leadership training around the world, I share a very simple principle: the truth that 24/7 worship was preceded in the life of David by the passion he expressed in Psalm 27:4. This was his life's mantra:

One thing I ask from the Lord, this only do I seek: that I may dwell in the house of the Lord all the days of my life, to gaze on the beauty of the Lord and to seek him in his temple (Psalm 27:4 NIV).

God is awakening this very same cry in many hearts in this hour. The burning passion of a Davidic heart for intimacy and worship is becoming rampant around the world. Many are catching the virus and it is transforming the church from the inside out! Intimacy and David's "one thing" is the ignition point for this global worship surge and the explosion of the worldwide worship movement. The prophecy of Amos concerning our day, later repeated by James in the New Testament, is occurring:

"I will return and rebuild David's fallen tent. Its ruins I will rebuild, and I will restore it, that the rest of mankind may seek the Lord, even all the Gentiles who bear my name" (Acts 15:16–17 NIV).

GLOBAL SATURATION

Malachi spoke of these times. The words of this Old Testament prophet validate and expound on the phenomena of Presence – and worship-based living. The entire globe is undergoing a saturation of worship that is increasing even as you read these words:

> For from the rising of the sun even to its setting, My name will be great among the nations, and in every place incense is going to be offered to My name, and a grain offering that is pure; for My name will be great among the nations," says the Lord of hosts (Malachi 1:11 NASB).

Malachi envisioned a day when "every place" would offer incense and flood the atmosphere of earth with the worship of God. This "incense" is the global sound of day and night worship 24/7 – 365. During the last few decades, we have witnessed a dramatic and unprecedented acceleration in the fulfillment of this prophetic word! The saturation of this sound and the rising of incense of praise are currently flooding the earth's atmosphere in one form or another from almost every people group and nation!

This transformational sound is not restricted to traditional Sunday morning church services or stale and sparsely attended Wednesday night prayer meetings. The awakening of the bride in the Presence of God is causing a barrage of worship to bombard slums, street corners, red-light districts, suburbs, cafés and prayer rooms all over the world. The sound is extending far beyond the four walls of the church, breaking open even the hardest ground and darkest hearts! "Every place" will become saturated with this sound! The lines are blurring as the sacred invades the secular with extravagant offerings from tribes, tongues, and nations pouring their finest praise at His feet! The overflow of love, affection, and passion from the church will overwhelm and astound the world!

Spirit of Encounter

An entire generation across planet earth is starving to know, feel, and experience the revelation of the beauty of Jesus. It is the only hope for the teenage cutter on the verge of suicide. It is the only *real* solution for radical Islamic terrorists who, under bondage of hate and demonic oppression, wreak havoc on the innocent. Persecuting terrorists turn into healing revivalists (Acts 9) and evil kings turn into prophesying worshippers (1 Samuel 10) – all fruit of a powerful encounter with worship!

This brings a new perspective and compelling reason to shift from boring, predictable, and powerless services of three fast songs, three slow songs, a sermonette, and closing prayer! More than a slick schedule or quick drive-by service, we must have an encounter with the Spirit of God marking our gatherings! We must create a place where He feels welcome and adored! An entirely new definition and depiction of "seeker sensitive" church is emerging. The secret is not in watering down our service to make it more palatable, but allowing the *true* Seeker of hearts, the Holy Spirit, to take total control! The presence of God will speak for Himself when He invades our churches, cities, and regions. The Holy Spirit is not so fragile that He requires our help through lengthy explanations. When people experience God's presence, they recognize it. When God shows up, He brings healing, deliverance, salvation and breakthrough. No place, people or nation remain the same!

A great responsibility falls on worshippers in this day to usher in this Spirit of Encounter by persistently releasing the knowledge of the glory of the Lord everywhere they go, through worship.

We have endless stories from around the world of hardline Muslims in Iraq, prostitutes in Amsterdam, head witches in Salem, and theology students at Harvard University having dramatic encounters leading to salvation by simply stepping into the atmosphere of His presence! There was no sermon, altar call or twisting their arm, they were overwhelmed with God's goodness, mercy, and beauty and could no longer withstand it! Even the most powerful professors, scholars, kings, and presidents will willingly and joyfully lay down their crowns at His feet! I truly believe God longs to release the spirit of encounter through worship like never before in our day to transform the world! We get to be the change agents He uses to declare and proclaim the truth of His glory, splendor, and fame across the land.

Habakkuk 2:14 declares, "For the earth will be filled with the knowledge of the glory of the Lord, as the waters cover the sea." I believe this verse is prophetically calling forth the day where worship literally floods the entirety of planet earth! We are not far away from that day, because the lost are hungry, desperate, and searching for the sound that carries the truth of a greater reality! Proverbs 29:18 states: "Where there is no revelation, people cast off restraint" (NIV). Unless churches, cities, and nations experience the revelation of the beauty, holiness, and might of God, there is no hope for a turnaround. That is why the worship and cultivating of a place for His Presence to reside is not a mere "strategy" or "part of the strategy," but THE STRATEGY for extending His Kingdom over all the earth! The tent pegs of David's tabernacle are being extended to usher in the greatest era of "beholding" all His glory, leading to "becoming" like Him.

THE MUZZLE IS COMING OFF

While leading worship at a typical Sunday morning church service not long ago, God downloaded to me a crazy vision. Due to the large attendance and multiple meetings that morning, there was a time restriction placed on worship and a tight schedule to fit everything into a compact service. In my younger and less mature day, the restrictions would have disturbed me and I might have tried to press the envelope during the meeting to extend the worship time! In other words, I might have tried to hijack the service to create more worship time!

As you can imagine, that method does not always work and only tends to create tension and isolation, even coming across as arrogant and dishonorable to those in leadership. It did not take me long to learn that God is not interested in empowering the ambition of independent renegades who disregard authority to bring a change. He longs for *dependent* sons and daughters, seated in places of honor, to become conduits of divine transformation. In addition, it is far better when God hijacks the service and we all sit back in amazement!

On this particular Sunday morning, I was content to believe that God could accomplish all He desired in the time allotted. I was sticking to the planned "order of service" and knew the Holy Spirit was not too fragile to move within those constraints.

The Lord downloaded an unusual vision to my spirit as I was leading the first song of worship that morning. The vision was of a very large and ferocious dog (similar to a K-9 police dog) with a muzzle firmly strapped around his mouth. The dog could not bark, bite, or even attack because the muzzle was holding him back. Instead, he was domesticated, silenced, and treated like a cute pet rather than a vicious dog. While I was praying through it, the Lord revealed to me that the dog represented the church of America in its current state. A "muzzle of silence" was restraining the church's sound, bite, and "attack." Because of this, the church was not operating in its intended function, and the world and dark spiritual powers viewed it as merely a "cute pet."

I prophesied that God longed to see the muzzle removed so the sound of worship and its "spiritual attack" could be released against darkness! I ended the vision and interpretation with a corporate prayer that God would "un-domesticate" our worship that morning, and He did just that! The worship time literally took over the service and a sound of unrestrained and uncontained praise exploded forth unlike any I have ever heard even to this day!

No Place Safe from THE SOUND

Armed with testimonies from around the world, our global Burn 24/7 tribe has been boldly declaring that "no place is safe anymore" from the sound of worship! It will infiltrate even the darkest dictator-led country! It will flood the streets, ghettos, slums, mosques, temples, and even hijack our predictable Sunday morning church meetings! It is a sound like "rushing waters" that cannot be contained or controlled!

Even with the explosion of Houses of Prayer, Furnaces of Worship, and stadium worship, I believe we have only seen the beginning of what God will do! This is just the intro to the first verse of a fresh, powerful, and dynamic song God is birthing in this generation! Praise and worship will spring forth from every nation, tribe, and tongue, and these early testimonies of breakthrough stir our hearts with hope for the fulfillment of Isaiah's words:

For as the soil makes the sprout come up and a garden causes seeds to grow, so the sovereign Lord will make righteousness and praise spring up before all nations (Isaiah 61:11 NIV).

IT'S A GLOBAL TAKE-OVER!

Since the humble and somewhat accidental beginnings of the Burn 24/7 movement first ignited on a college campus in Tulsa, Oklahoma, God has expanded it to over 120 cities and to some of the most unlikely places throughout the world! Who knew one breath of His Spirit on the glowing embers of our hearts during a midnight worship set in a stuffy dorm room could ignite an inferno that would spread like wildfire over the world!

Even as you read this, downtown flats in Minneapolis, Native American reservations across South Dakota, Hindu temples throughout India, makeshift tents perched in earthquake-ridden Haiti, red-light districts in Amsterdam, underground basements in Iran, and jungle huts of Indonesia are burning with a fire of worship that will not be extinguished. The sound of worship has ushered in waves of healings, salvations, breakthrough, and shifts in nations only the Presence of God can touch!

We are witnessing a prophetic word from the Lord coming to fruition in this season! He promised that a new breed of worshipping missionaries (or "musicianaries," as we call them) armed with this sound and reality of His overshadowing Presence would be unleashed in every nook and cranny of the earth where He is unknown and even despised. They are troubadours of worship—a new breed with a Davidic heart to live in the presence of God—who will not stop or be silenced until every molecule of the planet vibrates in song to the Lamb, who is worthy of all praise! They will not rest until worship is released and His name is made famous across the earth!

I will allow no sleep to my eyes, no slumber to my eyelids till I find a place for the Lord, a dwelling for the Mighty One of Jacob (Psalm 132: 4-5 NIV)

From our Fire and Fragrance training schools (partnered with YWAM) to our Burning Ones Internship and our global leadership summits, mission teams, conferences, and roundtables held all over the world, Burn 24/7 is determined to call forth and send out an influx of psalmists and worshippers to every corner of the earth! The time is coming when the frequencies of worship will be heard every place on earth that man inhabits! The invasion of this lovesick sound will infiltrate and bring forth a global transformation!

Who wants to join in the greatest heist in the history of the world? We are going to take the world back from the enemy and bring forth a complete atmospheric shift as darkness, oppression, and hopelessness surrender ownership to light, joy, and peace.

THE BATTLE FOR INTIMACY WITH THE LORD

PATRICIA KING

We engage in many spiritual battles throughout our Christian life, but I believe the greatest battle is the one for intimacy with the Lord, and worship is perhaps our single most important strategy. A productive, abundant, rewarding, and prosperous life in the Kingdom flows out of intimacy as His character and nature is formed in us. Because of its vital importance, it is no wonder that this is the area so often assaulted with distractions, insecurities, and disappointments.

HAVE YOU BEEN DISILLUSIONED AND DISAPPOINTED?

How often have you cried out for a deeper engagement with the Lord only to find emptiness and silence? How many times have you attempted to seek His face with all your heart and were pulled by distractions from every direction? How often have you left your devotional time disappointed, with your hope deferred?

This, my friend, describes the battle for intimacy. The enemy will attempt to pull us from the place that is the most critical to our life in God – the posture of "abiding in Him," our state of intimacy. One place he commonly attacks is personal and corporate worship. If he can keep us from entering into worship, he has achieved a major victory. Nothing is as precious as the times God inhabits our praises and we feel His presence.

After my good friend, Donna Bromley, returned from Mozambique where she spent time with Heidi Baker, we had an interesting conversation. Donna has always been a contender for intimacy with the Lord, and Heidi – well, in my eyes, Heidi is the champion in this area. She told me that while in Mozambique, Heidi said to her, "You have no idea the battle I have fought to maintain intimacy and to fight distraction." Intimacy – this is the battlefield, and distraction is the weapon he uses. Intimacy is what the enemy desires to steal from us more than anything else!

If the enemy can steal our intimacy with the Lord, he gets everything. Intimacy is the most important element of all in our Christian experience. However, when you understand the importance of something, you are willing to fight for it.

If the enemy can steal our intimacy with the Lord, he gets everything. Intimacy is the most important element of all in our Christian experience.

Even More Than a Feeling

What does intimacy look like… feel like… taste, sound, or smell like? A number of years ago when I felt extremely desperate to connect with the Lord in intimacy, I set apart an entire month to seek His face, and I did! The first ten days were grueling. I cried out to God with a deep longing for intimacy. I so passionately wanted to connect with Him that hour-by-hour I cried out to Him. I had felt distanced and distracted but now was my time to really connect. Although I called out to Him by the hour, confessed any sin that might be in the way, engaged in warfare, fasted, sang worship songs, and stayed up nights, I still could not sense the Lord's presence and I definitely did not feel intimate. I was utterly disappointed; I had never been so desperate and yet so empty and unfulfilled.

On the tenth day of faithfully seeking Him, I finally heard Him speak to my heart. I had been shouting through my tears, "Lord, where are You?" I was on my knees pounding the floor as I cried out in desperation. In His still, small voice He finally whispered, "I am right here. I've been here all the time. Why did you doubt?"

In that moment, I realized I had been in an "anxious *hoping* mode" rather than a "*faith* believing mode." I was hoping to be intimate but not believing to be. I was longing to *feel* His presence and desperately wanting Him close but I had overlooked *discerning* that He was there… all the time.

In that moment, Hebrews 11:6 came to mind, "Without faith it is impossible to please Him, for he who comes to God must believe that He is and that He is a rewarder of those who seek Him." I had failed to BELIEVE that He was right there and that He was meeting my heart's desire.

Faith is very different from hoping, and feeling is different from knowing. Hope is a desired expectation but faith is the "substance" of what we hope for – a knowing. Faith is so powerful that it becomes the "evidence" of what we are unable to "see" or feel because it is a confirmation beyond our senses (see Hebrews 11:1).

You Cannot Be Any More Intimate Than...

Over the next several months, He taught me more about the faith required to walk in intimacy. I remember once, crying out in worship, "Oh Lord, I want to be intimate with You." I was worshipping but felt nothing – empty and emotionless. This state made me feel condemned because I had always known the importance of intimacy, yet seldom felt it. I found myself striving in that worship session to *feel* something.

In the midst of my desperation, the Lord whispered, "You cannot be any more intimate with Me than you are right now." That took me by surprise because I did not *feel* intimacy, only emptiness. What did this mean?

He further revealed that His finished work on the cross was the deepest embrace that God could ever express to mankind. He said, "You are in Me and I am in you; we are one for eternity. You can't get any more intimate than that."

Immediately, I began to worship from a different perspective. Instead of *hoping* to be intimate, I began *believing* that I was. Not based on what I felt but on what I knew to be true. In that moment of clarity, the enemy tried to throw all his usual lies at me, "You are not loved by God... you are failing in your love for Him... He is disappointed with you because you are falling short of intimacy. Look at your friends, Donna and Heidi, they know how to be intimate, but not you. You lack what they have and you always will."

This time, however, the accusations did not stick because my intimacy with the Lord was not based on what I *felt* but rather on what was *true*. I pressed in and won that battle. However, the battle for intimacy is never a one-time fight – it is ongoing, and we need to know how to stand. The enemy will use many measures to distract us: condemnation, busyness, lack of focus, distractions with time priorities, and insecurities are merely a few. We have to learn how to fight through all of these things because this is our most important struggle – the battle for intimacy.

He said, "You are in Me and I am in you; we are one for eternity. You can't get any more intimate than that."

Following are some practical suggestions to assist you in the battle for intimacy:

- Believe – you are loved and cherished by God and He deeply longs for intimacy with you.

- Believe – you have been drawn into intimacy through the finished work of the cross. Let go of all striving and know that you already have intimacy; rest in that truth.

- Set aside time each day to – *worship* Him, love Him, pursue Him in faith. Schedule this time in your calendar, make it a priority, and do not let anything distract you from it.

- When distractions come during worship and intimacy – fight them off and do not allow discouragement. The enemy loves to discourage but you can press through into the "rest of faith." The Lord will honor your fight. Even if you spent a whole hour battling off distractions, it is better than not spending time with the Lord. He will see your efforts and reward you. Continue to battle, you will get a breakthrough! Keep focused on Jesus.

- Journaling helps you to keep focused – You might want to write down what He reveals to you as well as writing love letters to Him. Your declarations of love are precious to Him and you can use them as focal points of meditation weeks, months, and even years later.

- Abide in the Word – Spend time in the Scriptures each day. Allow the Lord to speak His heart to you through them.

- War in the heavenlies – Battle against the enemy's strategies through prayer and declaration of the Word. Declarations win the battle in the heavenlies before they hit the earth. Contend for intimacy for yourself, your family, and the rest of the body. What you sow into others you will reap.

- Throughout the day – look for opportunities to express love to the Lord. Make this a priority in life. He loves your love; it is a gift to Him. Express your love verbally, sing to Him both in your natural tongue and in your spirit language, and speak to Him in prayer throughout your day.

- Make intimacy your lifestyle – not something you engage in merely during devotions – intimacy is a way of life.

Declare War

The Scripture says in 2 Corinthians 2:14, "But thanks be to God, who always leads us in triumph in Christ, and manifests through us the sweet aroma of the knowledge of Him in every place." See? God has guaranteed your victory!

Christ has already won your battle for intimacy. Take that victory by faith and do not let go. Declare war against every distraction the enemy throws at you and make him sorry he ever tried. Put the pursuit of intimacy through worship, and other means, high on your list of priorities. It is your inheritance in Christ — your key to everything He created you to be... to do... and to have.

AUTHORS AND RESOURCES

NIC and RACHAEL BILLMAN and their four children live in Brazil and together lead Shores of Grace Ministries, a worship and missionary ministry. They take the love of Papa God and the power of the gospel to the prostitutes and transvestites on the streets of Brazil, where they have witnessed salvations, healings and miracles. They are also worship leaders and have released eight worship albums.

ROAR OF THE LION – Recorded in two of Nashville's premier studios. It is the perfect combination of studio quality and live passion. "As we worshipped, the studio was full of Papa's presence and it translates onto the album!" The album has seven tracks, including "Roar of the Lion" and "Bethany," a special song that came from an encounter that Nic and Rachael had during the time of the recording.

Available at www.shoresofgrace.com

JONATHAN WILLIAMS is the Director of The School of Worship for Teen Mania Ministries in Lindale, Texas. Jonathan's mission in life is to see worship leaders and musicians discipled into a lifestyle of worship and the Word of God. Jonathan has been able to lead worship and serve the body of Christ throughout the United States for over ten years.

INTO THE GLORY – This instrumental soaking album includes tracks such as "Awaiting the King" and "Realms of Glory," and is nearly an hour's worth of soaking music. This CD is a great tool to entering into the glory (the weighty presence) of our Father during personal devotion, meditation, prayer, or even simply relaxing. Each track is a unique time when Jonathan spent time with the Lord, and His glory came into the room as Jonathan was playing.

Available at www.jwworship.com

BISHOP JOSEPH GARLINGTON, Sr., PhD, is the senior pastor of Covenant Church of Pittsburgh, and is the presiding bishop over Reconciliation! Ministries International, an international network of churches and ministries. Bishop Garlington is an accomplished musician and recording artist, author and scholar. His work touches thousands through radio, a weekly TV broadcast called Something Fresh, national and international conferences, albums, books and articles.

WORSHIP: THE PATTERN OF THINGS IN HEAVEN – This book clearly describes the crucial roles that worship and praise are to play in the local church. It is anointed, refreshing, inspiring, and thoroughly Bible-based. It will enrich and transform your personal and corporate worship with the anointing that God ordained long ago when David sat alone before the shekinah presence of God. This book will become a reference work for leading pastors, worship leaders, and musicians around the world.

www.ccop.org

BRIAN WRIGHT grew up at Gateway Church (aka First Assembly of God) in Ashtabula, OH. Music has been a passion of Brian's since he was a teenager playing his guitar for his parents in ministry. Brian has held several leadership positions over the years, and has been the music minister at Gateway since 2000. His desire is for all to worship God in freedom – without fear of man – and encourages all to worship "on earth as it is in heaven."

THE WAVE is a time set apart to worship our Heavenly Father. No agendas, no preaching, no time limitations – nothing but worshipping the Creator of this world through music. Freedom reigns in The Wave service. Freedom to praise and worship the Perfect One, the Lamb who became the ultimate sacrifice. Our Lord delights in our seeking and pursuing Him. For more information, go to:

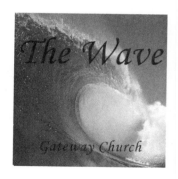

www.ashtabulawaveone.com

MICHAEL & ANGELA PINKSTON have been traveling the world leading, teaching, mentoring and writing in the area of worship for over a decade. During that time they also helped pioneer a ministry school in Alaska which focused much on worship, intercession and the prophetic. Currently in Albany, Oregon, the Pinkstons are worship leaders at their local fellowship, as well as traveling the country leading worship and teaching. Their songs and messages carry eternal realities of experience with Jesus.

THE PURSUIT: LIVE FROM ALBANY – Born out of deep personal times with the Father, it captures the essence of why we worship. Recorded live Easter weekend at Jesus Pursuit Church in Albany, Oregon, *The Pursuit* is an honest, raw, live worship album of nine original worship songs. Performed and arranged by the Jesus Pursuit worship team, the album has the sound and spirit that worship at Jesus Pursuit Church is known for throughout the Pacific Northwest and the nation.

www.thepinkstons.org

STEVE MITCHELL's worship is honest, prayerful, heartfelt, and carries with it a relentless pursuit to make contact with God. He views every corporate worship setting as a window of opportunity for divine encounters. He ministers at many conferences and churches throughout the country as a worship leader and psalmist. He and his wife Maria are on the leadership team at Metro Church in Saddle Brook, N.J., where he teaches, leads worship, and oversees the intercession and music ministry.

SONG OF THE ANGELS – If you read through the story of the prodigal son, you'll find it was his hunger that ultimately led him back to the father. You and I are spirit and there is a deep hunger in us for spirit food. The Bible speaks of a table that God has prepared for us so we can be "abundantly satisfied." The title track on this CD extends an invitation to that table.

www.stevemitchellworship.com

SANDY LOCKHART is a passionate worship leader and singer/songwriter based out of Victoria, BC, Canada. She has a strong gifting in prophetic and intercessory worship and seeks to follow the Holy Spirit in unlocking people and regions in the spirit realm. She desires to inspire and be a part of the revival generation that know who they are, are consumed by the presence of God, and change nations. She is married to Tim and they have four children.

WHERE I BELONG – a beautifully produced and inspiring collection of worship released September 2011. Many of the tracks could be described as modern day psalms that reflect Sandy's prayer conversations with the Father. This CD takes you on a passionate and intimate journey in the presence of God, refreshing and reminding you where you belong. It is now available through the XPmedia Canadian bookstore, iTunes, or directly from unlockedministries@gmail.com.

www.lionofjudah.ca

CALEB BRUNDIDGE is a passionate worship leader and lover of Jesus. Through the vehicle of DJ-led electronic worship music, Caleb leads believers into freedom in worship and praise by expressing adoration for Jesus through flag, song, and dance. This has included creating a new style of electronic music called ekstasis worship, which is intended to encourage believers to move as they enter a place of deep worship.

ENSIGN: A VISUAL EXPERIENCE IN FLAGGING – Journey with Caleb to scenic locations featured on this DVD. Explore the art of flagging and discover a new level of prophetic praise and worship as you listen to the original music soundtrack composed by Caleb himself.

www.calebbrundidge.com

ART LUCIER is the apostolic overseer of Kitimat Harvest Ministries International. He and his wife Heather are the pastors of The Harvest Church. They are also active members of the Canadian Prophetic Council. Together they lead worship at The Harvest as well as in outreaches throughout the area and around the nation. Harvest Ministries believes strongly in raising up the musicians of today and tomorrow as worshippers after God's own heart. Art is also a card-carrying Metis Aboriginal person of Canada.

FORGIVEN – Powerful music with a strong message. Some of the songs are: "Forgiven and Free," "Dance On It," "Father to the Fatherless," "Shine Forth Like the Sun," "K'chi Manitou." This album carries a First Nations flare. His albums, including, *Forgiven* and *Reviver - Rain Down*, can be purchased on iTunes.

www.harvestministriescanada.com

DENNIS SEE is founder and director of The Altar International House of Prayer in Meadville, PA. He is the director of the Pennsylvania House of Prayer Network, worship leader and speaker, as well as Kingdom business owner. He has traveled leading worship and speaking throughout the United States. His passion is to see day and night worship and prayer that will help sustain revival and awakening throughout Pennsylvania, the USA, and other nations.

DRAW ME TO INTIMACY will draw you into an intimate place of deep worship with the Lord. It will help you to know the Lord in a much deeper and personal way. It is a soaking CD with keyboard, violin, and vocals that flows from encountering God right into the secret place. At the end of the CD the spontaneous flow and prayer draws you even deeper into an encounter with Jesus. This is a must have CD for your devotional times. For more information visit:

www.thealtarihop.org

VINCE GIBSON is a pastor on the lead team for Abiding Glory Church in Knoxville, TN, and serves as the senior worship leader. He has a passion to lead others into the tangible presence of God and encourages the body to engage in the realms of the Spirit through worship. He longs to see the sounds of Heaven released here upon the earth to usher in the Kingdom. He has a Hegai mandate to prepare the bride of Christ for an encounter with the King and lead them to the chamber doors.

REVELATORY ABANDONED WORSHIP VOLUME 2 – In relationships, the spontaneous, unscripted moments are some of the most memorable times you experience. In these moments of worship together, we chase a "now" wind that's blowing. We are pulling on Heaven to come to earth on the spot. This album includes some of my favorite moments that we have captured live in worship. *RAW 2* and other products are available for download on iTunes.

www.vincegibsonmusic.com

JULIE MEYER is a prophetic singer and songwriter who carries the glory and the presence of God as an abandoned worshipper. Her passion is His presence as she trumpets the message of the Bridegroom preparing His bride! Julie has recorded several CDs and is the author of two books. Besides being a worship leader at International House of Prayer, Kansas City, she has led worship and spoken worldwide on hearing the voice of God, prophetic singing and worship.

PAINT YOUR PICTURE – Julie Meyer's artistic worship and musical creativity are evident in this album, in which Julie sings of her loving relationship with the Father. The powerful arrangements will move your heart, from full rock 'n' roll on the electric guitar to beautiful strums on the classical acoustic. The message is of hope and freedom. Julie's personal heart for Israel also comes through as she sings Jewish melodies and worships joyfully.

Available at: juliemeyer.com

SEAN FEUCHT is a husband, father, musician, speaker, writer, revivalist, and founder of the grassroots global worship, prayer and missions organization "Burn 24/7." His lifelong quest is to witness a generation of burning hearts arise in nations around the world with renewed faith, vision and sacrificial pursuit after the presence of God with reckless abandonment.

INCENSE RISE – These are the sounds of the Burn 24/7 movement. Burning with the fire of first love, our furnaces are flooding cities, regions and nations with incense of worship, praise and extravagant adoration. From midnight intercession anthems to early dawn spontaneous love songs, the stream of worship captured on this compilation is raw, pure and true to our DNA.

Sean has other CDs available, including "Your Presence is Enough," "Fire and Fragrance," and "Keep this Love Alive."

www.seanfeucht.com

PATRICIA KING is a respected minister of the gospel, successful owner of four flourishing businesses, and an inventive entrepreneur. She is an accomplished itinerant speaker, author, television host of "Everlasting Love," and media producer. She has given her life fully to Jesus Christ and to His Kingdom's advancement in the earth. She is the co-founder of XPmedia.com and overseer of XP Ministries.

SACRED TIME -SACRED PLACE

A Journal
An Invitation to Spend Time with God

This beautiful imitation leather journal has valuable tools to develop a rich devotional life. It includes practical guidelines to help you have a fruitful devotional time with Jesus, a plan to read the Bible in one year, and plenty of lined pages with a Bible Scripture at the bottom. Packaged in a gift box.

Available at the store at XPmedia.com

Available at the store at XPmedia.com

THE BRIDE LETTERS

A Revelation of Intimacy, Adoration and Warfare

Gary Galloway

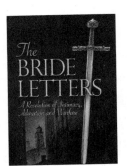

An invitation to take a thirty-day journey into the ravished heart of the Lord for his Bride. The author shares his own transparent journey in his quest for that place of deep and intimate communion with the Creator and the Lover of our soul. Includes interactive activities.

FINDING FATHER

A Journey into the Loving Arms of Daddy God

A.J. Jones

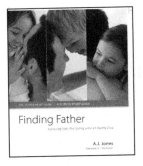

In this 12 week study guide, A.J. exposes the most common blockages that hinder our discovery of who God truly is and offers practical steps to overcome them. This guide is perfectly suited for an individual to use during their daily devotion time but is also a valuable resource for group Bible studies.

DOMINION SURGES

Prayers, Proclamations and Decrees for Breakthrough in your Life, Cities and Nations

Randy DeMain

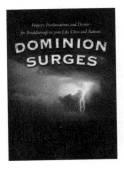

It's time to move forward, overcome and occupy your full inheritance! Dominion Surges will equip you to expand the dominion of the King of Kings in your personal life and where you live. It models how to combine the Word, worship, the prophetic, and prayer into one, unfolding your beliefs into words of action, intent, and pursuit. Get ready to experience breakthrough!

Available at the store at XPmedia.com

JOURNEY INTO THE GLORY!

In *Powerful Encounters in the God-Realm*, you will accompany several very credible witnesses on their spiritual journeys and experiences in the glory and the supernatural. As they share insights from their moments in the supernatural, you will be awed as you learn what they learned. Yet, most importantly, you will find insights that will guide you to that sphere of supernatural encounter. Patricia King says, "Every Christian has an invitation to experience the glories of that realm NOW!" Read, enjoy, and then…encounter!

CONTRIBUTING AUTHORS

Georgian Banov

Kaye Beyer

Stacey Campbell

Randy DeMain

Faytene Grasseschi

Joan Hunter

Patricia King

Julie Meyer

Joshua Mills

Jerame Nelson

Matt Sorger

Samuel Robinson

Katie Souza

Darren Wilson

Additional copies of this book may be purchased through the authors' ministries, bookstores and at the store at XPmedia.com

For wholesale discounts, contact: usaresource@xpmedia.com. For Canadian bulk orders, contact: resource@xpmedia.com.

This book and other books published by XP Publishing are also available to bookstores through Anchor Distributors.

www.XPpublishing.com

Christian Services Association